PATCHWORK PICNIC

Suzette Halferty and Nancy J. Martin

Martingale
& COMPANY

WOODINVILLE, WASHINGTON

Credits

President . . . . Nancy J. Martin
CEO/Publisher . . . . Daniel J. Martin
Associate Publisher . . . . Jane Hamada
Editorial Director . . . . Mary V. Green
Editorial Project Manager . . . . Tina Cook
Technical Editor . . . . Darra Williamson
Copy Editor . . . . Ellen Balstad
Design and Production Manager . . . . Stan Green
Illustrator . . . . Laurel Strand
Cover and Text Designer . . . . Trina Stahl
Photographer . . . . Brent Kane

Martingale & COMPANY

That Patchwork Place®

That Patchwork Place is an imprint of Martingale & Company.

Patchwork Picnic
© 2001 by Suzette Halferty and Nancy J. Martin

Martingale & Company
20205 144th Avenue NE
Woodinville, WA 98072-8478 USA
www.martingale-pub.com

Printed in Hong Kong

06 05 04 03 02 01   8 7 6 5 4 3 2 1

Mission Statement

We are dedicated to providing quality products and service
by working together to inspire creativity and to
enrich the lives we touch.

Library of Congress Cataloging-in-Publication Data

Halferty, Suzette.
   Patchwork picnic / Suzette Halferty and Nancy J. Martin.
      p. cm.
   ISBN 1-56477-342-6
   1. Patchwork—Patterns. 2. Appliqué—Patterns. 3. Picnicking. 4. Outdoor cookery. 5. Patchwork quilts. 6. Seasons in art. I. Martin, Nancy,-
II. Title.
TT835.M38297 2001
746.46'041—dc21
                                     00–065359

CONTENTS

INTRODUCTION · 5

TIPS FOR SUCCESSFUL PICNICS · 7

LUNCH IN THE HERB GARDEN · 9

    Recipe: Chicken-with-Herbal-Spread Sandwiches · 9

    Quilt: Herbal Jewel · 10

SPRING PICNIC IN THE GARDEN · 15

    Recipe: Poached Salmon with Mango Salsa · 15

    Quilt: Garden Bee Loved · 16

    Recipe: Picnic Asparagus · 20

CHILD'S TEA PARTY · 25

    Recipe: Sugar Posy Cookies · 25

    Quilt: Posy Pots · 26

FATHER'S DAY PICNIC · 31

    Recipe: Grilled Meat with Rich and Savory Sauce · 31

    Quilt: Cabin Fever · 32

CONCERT IN THE PARK · 41

    Recipe: Summer Fruit Salad · 41

    Quilt: Blue Willow · 42

    Companion Project: Silverware Carrier · 47

FOURTH OF JULY · 49

    Recipe: Fresh Tomato Tart · 49

    Quilt: Stars and Stripes · 50

    Companion Project: Casserole Carrier · 59

DINNER ON THE DECK · 63

    Recipe: Sand Dune Salad · 63

    Quilt: Seashore Dreamin' · 64

TAILGATE PARTY · 71

    Recipe: Picnic Potato Salad · 71

    Quilt: Market Square · 72

    Recipe: Butternut Bisque · 76

    Companion Project: Lined Picnic Basket · 78

A DRIVE IN THE COUNTRY · 81

    Recipe: Sweet Hazelnut Pound Cake · 81

    Quilt: Indian Summer · 82

TREE-CUTTING PICNIC · 87

    Recipe: Tree Hunter's Stew · 87

    Quilt: Christmas Tree Farm · 88

    Recipes: Mulled Wine and Spiced Cider · 93

NEW YEAR'S EVE BY THE FIRE · 97

    Recipe: Potted Beef Pâté · 97

    Quilt: Champagne Elegance · 98

HOUSEWARMING FOR A HOUSE-IN-PROGRESS · 105

    Recipe: Builder's Bruschetta · 105

    Quilt: Dream House · 106

VALENTINE PICNIC · 113

    Recipe: Lovers' Tart · 113

    Quilt: Sweetheart Trellis · 114

QUILTMAKING BASICS · 119

ACKNOWLEDGMENTS · 128

THE WORD "PICNIC" calls to mind a casual meal eaten outside on a sunny day and featuring a variety of transportable foods. Expressions such as "tailgate picnic," "fireside picnic," "picnic lunch," and "picnic in the park" are part of our standard vocabulary. In fact, picnic has such a pleasant connotation that a difficult job is often referred to as "no picnic"! Although picnics are typically thought of as summertime activities, they are also great for fall outings or activities like a winter tree-cutting excursion—just pack some hot food and bundle up! If bad weather or other obstacles arise, the spirit of a picnic can also be re-created indoors. A romantic picnic for two can be served on a rug in front of the fireplace or some other cozy spot inside your home.

How did the concept of a picnic emerge? Historians trace the picnic to Victorian England, whose citizens enjoyed outdoor leisure activities. As with all of their pursuits, Victorians required special gear for a picnic: wicker hampers outfitted with drawers and compartments, and collapsible safari chairs, tea tables, and butler's trays. Often these picnics took place in a garden or glade some miles from the city, with horse-drawn carriages or boats transporting both picnickers and food. The compartmentalized hampers protected breakables and prevented food from spilling. They also helped ensure that every essential item was included, for as the hamper was packed, one could check that each specific compartment was filled.

British ingenuity also developed the Thermos bottle in 1896, when a British scientist named Sir James Dewar invented a flask which kept things hot or cold without heat or refrigeration. However, the Germans were the first to patent this invention and called it "Thermos," after the Greek word meaning "hot."

Around the turn of the century, Americans did their share to develop special items for use while picnicking. For example, they designed wicker-wrapped bottles and jugs to keep glass

from shattering, and divided picnic baskets so nothing could shift, spill, or drip. One notable manufacturer was the Hawkeye Basket Company of Burlington, Iowa, which developed a basket with separate storage for food and ice. In addition, the Hawkeye basket was insulated with a tin lining that kept ants out, adding another ingenious—and welcome—feature. The picnic basket shown in the photo above was patented by the Hawkeye Basket Company on November 4, 1902.

By the 1920s, automobiles had become more common, and so had auto excursions into the countryside. Since fast food and roadside restaurants were not yet available, a new line of picnicware developed, geared especially for motorists. The unwieldy wicker models popular at the turn of the century were replaced by cheaper and lighter metal baskets. Some of these red plaid and green plaid tin baskets can still be found because they were produced in record numbers. Variations included a woven basket with a plaid tin-tray top, and the aptly named "auto basket," whose handles hooked right over the car seat.

Matching red or green plaid thermos bottles and beverage coolers with spouts were also available. One early thermos bottle featured a Ball canning jar, complete with metal top and enclosed in a metal casing. In 1955, the green plaid Cape Cod cooler became a standard for picnic excursions. Its handy spigot served many gallons of lemonade.

Picnics are no longer restricted to the "down home" variety that features red-checkered tablecloths, hot dogs, hamburgers, and potato salad. While this type of traditional picnic will always be popular, more elegant picnics that feature all manner of tasty, elaborate fare are coming into their own as well.

Most people would agree that picnics, no matter how simple or elaborate, are just plain fun and certainly an easy way to entertain. So prepare your guest list and create clever invitations that feature seed packets, flags, pressed flowers, or other items related to your picnic theme. Our goal in *Patchwork Picnic* is to present some enjoyable, picnic-style events that are designed to be served on picnic-sized quilts. The book follows the four

seasons, with each featuring a variety of seasonal picnics and recipes to try, and a theme or color-related quilt to make. We think you'll find the quilts fun and easy due to their relatively small size (most are approximately 60" square) and the quick piecing and fusing techniques used in their construction.

Each of our picnic quilts is meant to be used both indoors and out. You can use your picnic quilt as a tablecover at any time of the year. During the warm-weather months, you can spread it on the ground outdoors for guests to sit upon while enjoying their picnic treats. In either case, you may want to put an inexpensive tablecloth or piece of fabric under the quilt to keep the reverse side from getting soiled.

Picnic quilts provide warmth and cheer at cold-weather picnics, too. They are great for bundling up in around the campfire or while riding home from an outdoor event.

If you prefer your picnic quilt to be decorative rather than functional, simply hang it near the picnic site for an additional splash of color. However you use these Patchwork Picnic quilts, they are certain to make your picnic more festive.

Choosing a Site

TAKE CARE to situate your outdoor picnic in a shady spot! Not only does shade protect the quilt's fabrics from fading in the sunlight, but it also ensures the comfort of the picnickers and helps keep the food from spoiling.

Bug Off

To ENSURE a comfortable outdoor picnic, be sure to take along plenty of bug repellent. If you'd rather not use pesticides, carry along a citronella candle to burn, or try using herbal preventatives. Many scents that are pleasant to people, such as lavender, marigold, rosemary, eucalyptus, and bay, will help to keep the bugs away. For instance, fill plant misters with a solution of weak mint tea to use as a spray to repel mosquitoes. Sprigs of fresh mint tied to overhanging branches also help keep mosquitoes away, while combining mint and basil in a floral centerpiece helps repel flies. Keep ants at bay by surrounding your picnic with tansy or catnip. While they may not be as effective as commercial products, these natural remedies are helpful, and they are kinder to the environment.

Setting the Table

DON'T SPOIL a special picnic by using plain white paper plates and plastic forks: picnicware has come a long way since the 1950s! If you are concerned about breakage or wish to make cleanup extra simple, visit a party store and see the wide variety of colorful (and durable) plates, utensils, and napkins available in many different designs.

You might also consider bringing traditional table settings outdoors for your picnics. Not only is this less costly than purchasing settings for each picnic, but it is also environment-friendly because you wash and reuse the items rather than discard them. Because picnics are special, consider carefully packing china, ironstone, or pottery dishes to set the mood. Be creative as you match the flatware to the dishes, either contrasting the mood or following a theme.

No matter which option you choose for serving your picnic, be sure to bring along plenty of oversized napkins or even dishtowels!

Safeguarding Food Temperatures

MAINTAINING THE proper temperature for your food—both hot and cold—is an important safety factor for any picnic. Use well-sealed, insulated containers or thermoses to keep food hot or cold.

While wicker and woven picnic baskets are definitely more appealing than ice chests, perishables and foods requiring refrigeration should be carried in a cooler with lots of ice or artificial ice packs inside. Use your decorative baskets to transport dishes, tablecloths, utensils, and any food or beverages normally kept at room temperature.

CELEBRATE THE WARM, *sunny days of spring with a refreshing outdoor luncheon set amid the fresh fragrances of an herb garden. The pungent herbal rows delight the senses while providing the perfect seasonings for your springtime menu. You can make your picnic portable by using the following recipe; then head for the herb farm or nearby country meadow. You'll enjoy collecting fabrics for our charming "Herbal Jewel" picnic quilt, the perfect complement to your springtime outing. The pretty leaf appliqués and embroidered embellishments capture the pleasure of selecting herbs to grace your simple feast.*

Chicken-with-Herbal-Spread Sandwiches

HERBAL SPREAD

1 cup fresh basil leaves, packed*
¼ cup fresh tarragon leaves*
2 cloves garlic
1 teaspoon black pepper
1 teaspoon salt
½ cup olive oil
½ cup balsamic vinegar
½ cup parmesan cheese
½ cup pine nuts

INGREDIENTS FOR SANDWICH

4 boneless chicken breasts, grilled and sliced
2 tablespoons pine nuts
1 grilled red pepper, cut into 4 slices
4 small French rolls, cut in half
8 thin slices mozzarella cheese
Optional: fresh basil leaves

*Don't be afraid to experiment and substitute for these herbs depending upon your taste and the season.

PLACE all herbal-spread ingredients in a food processor or blender and process until smooth. Makes approximately 1¼ cups of herbal spread.

Mix grilled chicken and pine nuts with herbal spread. Place grilled red-pepper slices on rolls, followed by chicken mixture. Top with mozzarella slices and fresh basil leaves if desired.

YIELD: 4 SANDWICHES.

Herbal Jewel

HERBAL JEWEL
by Suzette Halferty, Carnation, Washington, 2000. Quilted by Suzie Hostetler, Millersburg, Ohio.

Finished Size: 60" x 60"

Materials

44"-wide fabric

- 2½ yds. dark green fabric for vine and leaf appliqués (inner panel)
- Scraps of assorted pink fabrics for berry appliqués
- 2¾ yds. yellow print for appliqué panels and outer border
- ¼ yd. medium green subtle print for narrow sashing
- ½ yd. floral print for wide sashing
- 1¾ yds. light green fabric for leaf and vine appliqués (border)
- ¼ yd. pink solid or subtle print for inner border
- 3¾ yds. fabric for backing
- 26" x 26" square of fabric for bias binding
- 64" x 64" square of lightweight batting
- Green embroidery floss

Cutting

All measurements include ¼"-wide seam allowances.

From the dark green fabric, cut:

- 3 bias strips, each ¾" x 60", for panel vines*

From the yellow print, cut:

- 3 strips, each 8½" x 40½", for appliqué panels
- 4 strips, each 9¼" x 63", on the *lengthwise* grain for outer border

From the medium green subtle print, cut:

- 4 strips, each 1½" x 40½", for narrow sashing

From the floral print, cut:

- 2 strips, each 6½" x 40½", for wide sashing

From the light green fabric, cut:

- 8 bias strips, each ¾" x 30", for border vines*

From the pink fabric, cut:

- 2 strips, each 1½" x 40½", for inner border
- 2 strips, each 1½" x 42½", for inner border

*Refer to page 125 for guidance in cutting bias strips.

Note: *Refer to "Quiltmaking Basics" on pages 119–127 for guidance as needed with all basic quiltmaking techniques.*

Appliquéing and Assembling the Panels

1. Use the patterns on page 13 to make templates for appliqué pieces A–K. Trace the templates and cut from the dark green fabric: 6 each of pieces A, F, and H; 3 each of pieces C, D, E, and G; and 18 of piece B. Trace and cut from the assorted pink scraps a total of: 24 of piece I, 15 of piece J, and 18 of piece K.

2. Refer to "Bias-Strip Appliqué" on page 121, and use the ¾" x 60" *dark* green bias strips to make 3 vines. Each finished vine should measure a scant ¼" x 60".

3. Fold each 8½" x 40½" yellow panel in half vertically and horizontally to find its center point; crease lightly.

4. Pin or baste the appliqués in place as shown at right. Use your preferred method to appliqué the leaves, vines, and berries to the panels. Make 3 panels.

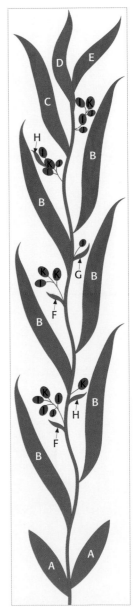

Appliqué Placement Diagram

5. Use 2 strands of green embroidery floss and an outline stitch to embroider the berry stems as shown.

6. Refer to the assembly diagram below and the color photo on page 10. Arrange the appliquéd panels, 1½" x 40½" medium green narrow sashing strips, and 6½" x 40½" wide floral sashing strips as shown. Sew the panels and sashing strips together. Press seams away from the appliqué panels.

Assembly Diagram

APPLIQUÉING AND ADDING THE BORDERS

1. Use the pattern on page 13 to make a template for appliqué pattern L. Trace the template and cut 104 of piece L from the light green fabric.

2. Use the ¾" x 30" *light* green bias strips to make 8 vines. Each finished vine should measure a scant ¼" x 30".

3. Fold each 9¼"-wide outer border strip in half vertically and horizontally to find its center point; crease lightly.

4. Refer to the border appliqué placement diagram below and the color photo on page 10. Pin or baste the appliqués in place as shown. Use your preferred method to appliqué the vines and leaves to the panels.

5. Use 2 strands of green embroidery floss and an outline stitch to embroider the leaf stems.

Border Appliqué Placement Diagram

6. Sew a 1½" x 40½" pink inner border strip to opposite sides of the quilt. Press seams toward the border strips. Sew a 1½" x 42½" pink inner border strip to the top and bottom of the quilt. Press.

7. Sew the 9¼" x 63" appliquéd borders to the quilt, mitering the corners as described on page 122. Press seams toward the outer border.

FINISHING

1. Mark the quilt top with a design of your choice.

2. Layer the quilt top with batting and backing; baste.

3. Hand or machine quilt as desired.

4. Trim the backing and batting even with the edges of the quilt top. Cut 2¼"-wide bias strips from the 26" square of binding fabric for a total of approximately 250" of bias binding. Sew the binding to the quilt.

5. Make and attach a label to the quilt.

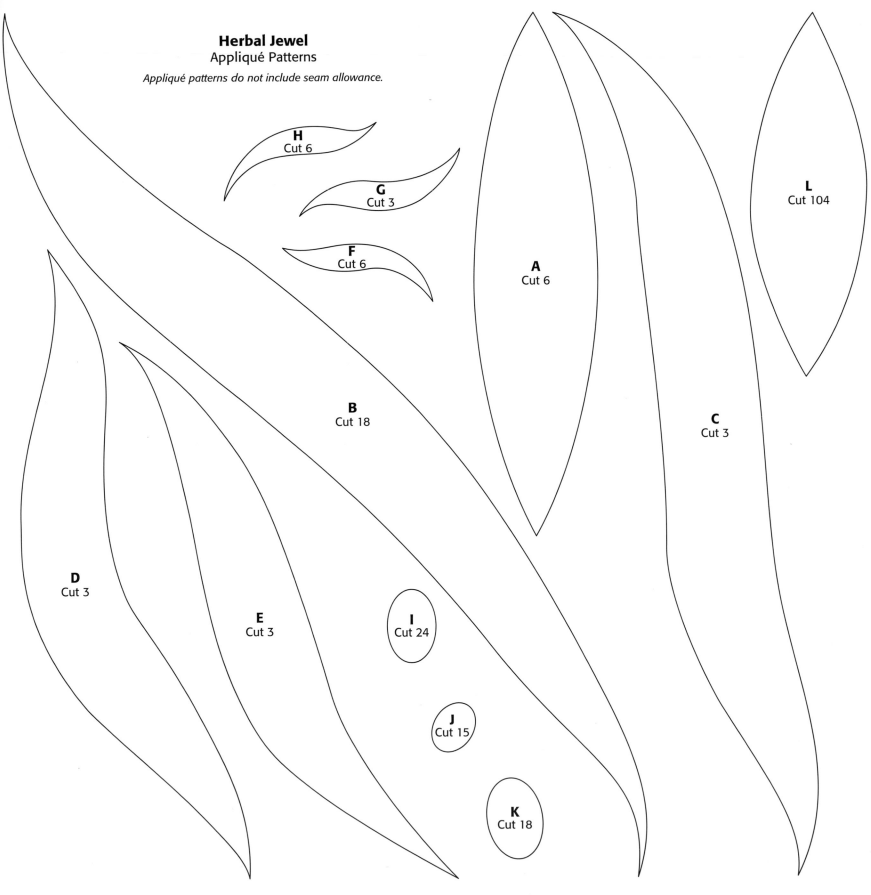

Herbal Jewel
Appliqué Patterns

Appliqué patterns do not include seam allowance.

H
Cut 6

G
Cut 3

F
Cut 6

A
Cut 6

L
Cut 104

B
Cut 18

C
Cut 3

D
Cut 3

E
Cut 3

I
Cut 24

J
Cut 15

K
Cut 18

*S*PRINGTIME CONJURES UP *youthful memories of flying kites and chasing dragonflies. What a treat to finally sit out-*
doors, enjoying the spring run of fresh salmon, the scent of freshly cut grass, and the chirping of newborn birds!
As the buzzing bees pollinate the many spring blossoms, you'll enjoy capturing the season with our "Garden Bee Loved"
quilt. Whether you choose a collection of elegant floral fabrics or select bright and cheery children's theme prints, you'll find this quilt
goes together quickly with its beehive and bumblebee appliqués and charming picket-fence border.

Poached Salmon with Mango Salsa

POACHED SALMON

Four 6-ounce salmon fillets
2 cups white wine or champagne
2 cups water
2 cloves garlic, mashed
1 teaspoon salt
1 bay leaf

POACH salmon fillets for 6 minutes in mixture of wine, water, garlic, salt, and bay leaf; remove salmon from liquid and refrigerate.

MANGO SALSA

1 avocado, diced
Juice of 1 lime
¼ cup sugar
2 tablespoons white wine vinegar
2 tablespoons olive oil
1 papaya, peeled, seeded, and diced
1 mango, peeled, seeded, and diced
½ cup small red onion, diced
¼ cup red pepper, diced
2 tablespoons fresh cilantro, chopped

DRIZZLE avocado with lime juice to prevent browning. Add all other salsa ingredients and place in a large resealable plastic bag. Top each cold poached salmon fillet (see directions for poached salmon opposite) with a generous helping of salsa.

YIELD: 6 SERVINGS.

Garden Bee Loved

GARDEN BEE LOVED

by Suzette Halferty, Carnation, Washington, 2000. Quilted by Emma Shetler, Charm, Ohio.

Finished Quilt Size: 60" x 60"
Finished Block Size: 6⅜" square

Materials

44"-wide fabric

- ½ yd. blue solid or subtle print for blocks and alternate squares
- ½ yd. small-scale, yellow floral print for blocks and picket-fence border
- ½ yd. floral print #1 for blocks, alternate squares, and picket-fence border
- ¼ yd. floral print #2 for blocks and alternate squares
- ½ yd. green floral print for setting triangles
- ⅜ yd. yellow print for inner border
- 1 yd. green print for picket-fence border
- 1 yd. white print for picket-fence border
- ⅝ yd. light print for corner squares
- ¼ yd. brown subtle print for beehive trim appliqués
- ½ yd. gold solid for bee and beehive appliqués
- ¼ yd. black solid for bee stripe and beehive door appliqués
- ½ yd. white solid for bee wing appliqués
- 3¾ yds. fabric for backing
- 26" x 26" square of fabric for bias binding
- 1 yd. lightweight fusible web
- Black, light blue, and medium brown embroidery floss
- 64" x 64" square of lightweight batting

I N ANCIENT TIMES, HONEY WAS CONSIDERED ONE OF THE FOODS OF THE GODS. HONEY ASSUMES THE FLAVOR OF THE FLOWERS FROM WHICH BEES GATHER THEIR NECTAR. YOU CAN EASILY CHANGE THE FLAVOR OF HONEY TO SUIT YOUR FANCY. SIMPLY WARM IT ON THE STOVE AND ADD YOUR FAVORITE FLAVORING, SUCH AS BERRIES, GINGER, OR LAVENDER.

Cutting

All measurements include ¼"-wide seam allowances.

From the blue fabric, cut:
- 6 squares, each 6⅞" x 6⅞", for alternate squares
- 3 squares, each 7¼" x 7¼". Cut each square once diagonally to make 6 triangles for blocks.

From the small-scale, yellow floral print, cut:
- 6 squares, each 7¼" x 7¼". Cut each square once diagonally to make 12 triangles for blocks.
- 40 squares, each 2½" x 2½", for picket-fence border

From floral print #1, cut:
- 2 squares, each 7¼" x 7¼". Cut each square once diagonally to make 4 triangles for blocks. You will have 1 triangle left over.
- 3 squares, each 6⅞" x 6⅞", for alternate squares
- 40 squares, each 2½" x 2½", for picket-fence border

From floral print #2, cut:
- 2 squares, each 7¼" x 7¼". Cut each square once diagonally to make 4 triangles for blocks. You will have 1 triangle left over.
- 3 squares, each 6⅞" x 6⅞", for alternate squares

From the green floral print, cut:
- 4 squares, each 10¼" x 10¼". Cut each square twice diagonally to make 16 setting triangles.

From the yellow print, cut:
- 2 strips, each 2½" x 36½", for inner border
- 2 strips, each 2½" x 40½", for inner border

From the green print, cut:
- 40 rectangles, each 2½" x 10½", for picket-fence border

From the white print, cut:
- 40 rectangles, each 2½" x 10½", for picket-fence border

From the light print, cut:
- 4 squares, each 10½" x 10½", for corner squares

NOTE: *Refer to "Quiltmaking Basics" on pages 119–127 for guidance as needed with all basic quiltmaking techniques.*

MAKING AND ASSEMBLING THE BLOCKS

1. Sew a blue triangle and a small-scale, yellow floral-print triangle together to make a square. Press seam toward the blue triangle. Make 6.

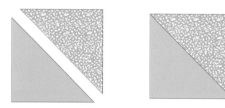

Make 6.

2. Sew a floral-print #1 triangle to a small-scale, yellow floral-print triangle to make a square. Press seam toward the darker triangle. Make 3.

Make 3.

3. Sew a floral-print #2 triangle to a small-scale, yellow-print triangle to make a square. Press seam toward the darker triangle. Make 3.

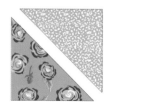

Make 3.

4. Arrange the blocks from steps 1–3; the 6⅞" blue, floral #1, and floral #2 alternate squares; and the green floral-print setting triangles in diagonal rows as shown.

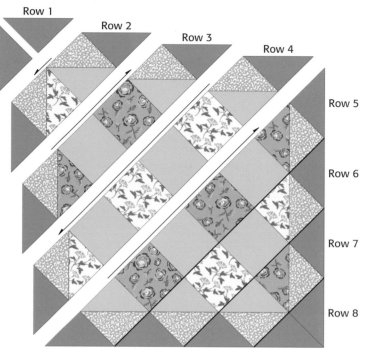

Row 1
Row 2
Row 3
Row 4
Row 5
Row 6
Row 7
Row 8

Assembly Diagram

5. Pin and then sew the blocks, squares, and setting triangles to make 8 diagonal rows. Press seams in opposite directions from row to row. Sew the rows together; press.

6. Sew a 2½" x 36½" yellow inner border strip to opposite sides of the quilt. Press seams toward the border strips. Repeat to sew a 2½" x 40½" yellow inner border strip to the top and bottom of the quilt; press.

Assembling the Border

1. Draw a diagonal line from corner to corner on the wrong side of each 2½" floral-print #1 square. Place a floral-print #1 square right sides together with each 2½"x 10½" green rectangle as shown. Stitch on the drawn line, and trim away the excess. Press toward the small triangle. Make 40.

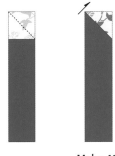

Make 40.

2. Repeat step 1 to mark and then sew a 2½" small-scale, yellow floral-print square to each 2½" x 10½" white rectangle as shown; press. Make 40.

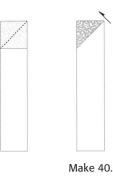

Make 40.

3. Sew units from steps 1 and 2 together in pairs as shown. Press seams toward the step 1 units. Make 40.

Make 40.

4. Sew 10 units from step 3 to make a border unit as shown. Press seams to one side. Make 4 border units.

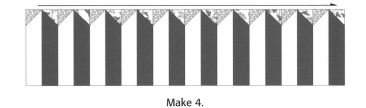

Make 4.

5. Refer to the color photo on page 16. Sew a border unit from step 4 to opposite sides of the quilt, taking care to position the "picket fence" as shown. Press seams toward the inner border strips.

6. Sew a 10½" light-print corner square to each end of the remaining border units. Press seams toward the corner squares.

7. Sew a border unit from step 6 to the top and bottom of the quilt, taking care to position the "picket fence" as shown in the photo; press.

Carry a jar of water in your picnic basket for arranging freshly picked wild flowers. (If your picnic is in a state park or campground, be sure that flower picking is permitted!) The vintage bottle carrier shown here makes the perfect holder for canning jars full of fresh-cut flowers. ❧

Picnic Asparagus

1 pound fresh asparagus
½ cup thinly sliced red pepper
¼ cup olive oil
Zest and juice of 1 orange
2 tablespoons cilantro, chopped
1 tablespoon garlic, minced
2 tablespoons brown sugar
2 teaspoons fresh minced ginger

Cook asparagus in boiling water for 6 to 8 minutes; drain and place in ice water to cool. Combine remaining ingredients in large resealable plastic bag and add the cooled asparagus to marinate for at least ½ hour.

Yield: 6 servings.

Adding Appliqués and Embroidery

1. Referring to "Fusible-Web Appliqué" on page 120, prepare the brown print and gold, black, and white solid fabrics for fusing.

2. Use the patterns on pages 22–23 to make templates for appliqué pieces A–L. Use the templates to trace the following appliqués from the bonded fabric: 24 of piece A from the white solid; 12 each of pieces B, D, and E and 4 of piece L from the black solid; 4 each of pieces G–K from the brown print; and 12 of piece C and 4 of piece F from the gold solid.

3. Refer to appliqué placement diagram #1 below and the color photo on page 16. Follow the manufacturer's instructions to fuse 3 bees (appliqués A–E) in alphabetical order to each picket-fence border.

4. Use an outline stitch and 3 strands of black embroidery floss to embroider antennae on each bee and to outline each appliqué shape on the bees' bodies. Use 3 strands of light blue embroidery floss and a buttonhole stitch to outline the bees' wings. Use a long running stitch and 3 strands of black embroidery floss to embroider swirls to indicate the bees' flight paths.

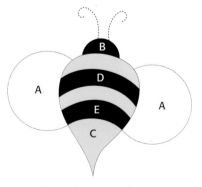

Appliqué Placement Diagram #1

5. Refer to appliqué placement diagram #2 on page 21 and the color photo on page 16. Fuse a beehive (appliqués F–L) to each corner square.

6. Use an outline stitch and 3 strands of brown embroidery floss to outline the beehive markings. Use an outline stitch and 3 strands of black embroidery floss to outline each beehive and beehive door.

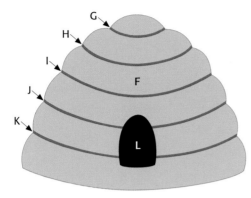

Appliqué Placement Diagram #2

FINISHING

1. Mark the quilt top with the design of your choice.

2. Layer quilt top with batting and backing; baste.

3. Hand or machine quilt as desired.

4. Trim the backing and batting even with the edges of the quilt top. Cut 2¼"-wide bias strips from the 26" square of binding fabric, for a total of approximately 250" of bias binding. Sew the binding to the quilt.

5. Make and attach a label to the quilt.

A CHEERFUL CHILD'S QUILT CAN BE MADE FROM THE "GARDEN BEE LOVED" QUILT INSTRUCTIONS (PAGES 16–21). SUBSTITUTE BRIGHT, HAPPY COLORS FOR THE SOFT PASTEL FLORALS, AND ELIMINATE THE BEE AND BEEHIVE APPLIQUÉS. INSTEAD, APPLIQUÉ SMALL CIRCLES AT THE INTERSECTIONS OF THE SQUARES, AS SHOWN IN THE PHOTO BELOW.

GARDEN BEE LOVED COMPANION QUILT
by Suzette Halferty, Carnation, Washington, 1999.
Quilted by Emma Shetler, Charm, Ohio.

Garden Bee Loved
Appliqué Patterns

Appliqué patterns do not include seam allowance.

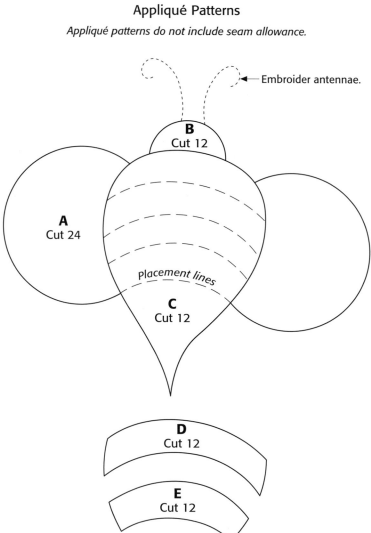

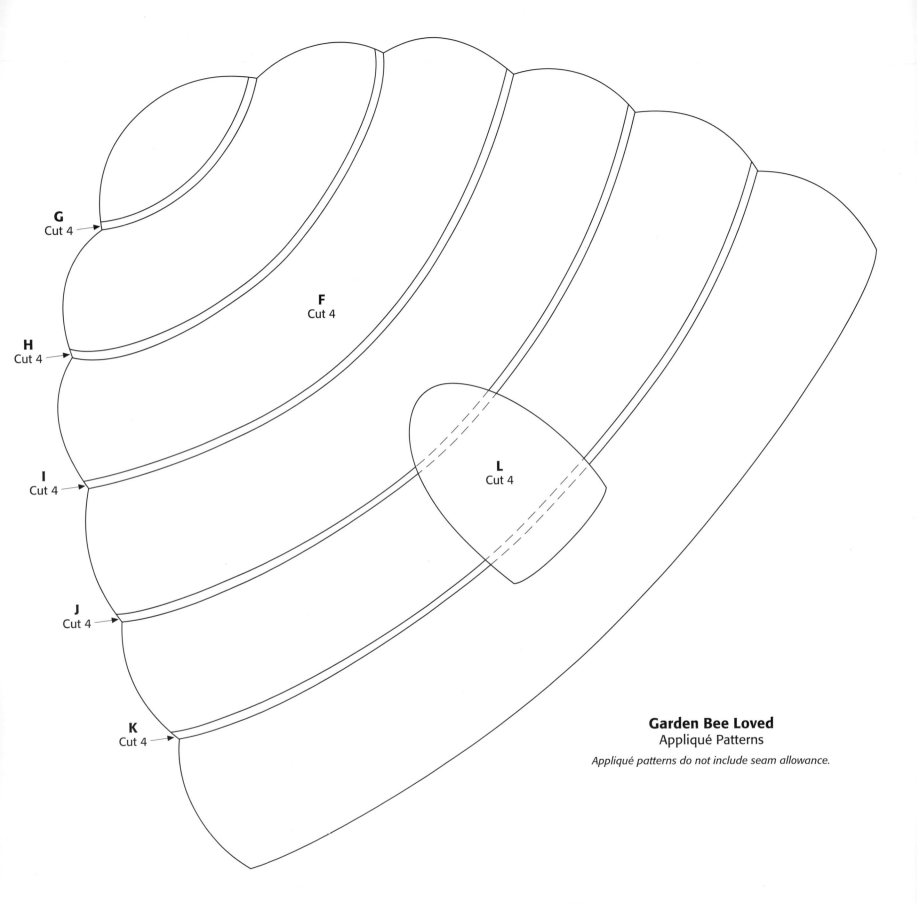

G
Cut 4

F
Cut 4

H
Cut 4

I
Cut 4

L
Cut 4

J
Cut 4

K
Cut 4

Garden Bee Loved
Appliqué Patterns

Appliqué patterns do not include seam allowance.

*A*LTHOUGH WE ENJOY *the profusion of pretty daffodils, colorful tulips, and blossoming trees, springtime often finds us indoors with rain showering against the windowpanes. Porches and hallways overflow with colorful little rubber boots, wet raincoats, and dripping umbrellas. What a perfect time to enjoy a cozy tea party or indoor picnic, bringing all of spring's pretty palette inside.*

"Posy Pots," a cheery, colorful scrappy quilt, echoes the April showers/May flowers time of year. Its pleasing combination of simple piece-work and appliqués, comfortable 1930s reproduction prints, and mix-and-match buttons lends a potful of charm to this springtime treasure.

Sugar Posy Cookies

INGREDIENTS

½ pound (2 sticks) unsalted butter
1 cup granulated sugar
1 egg
1 tablespoon milk or cream
1 teaspoon vanilla
1 teaspoon baking soda
1 teaspoon baking powder
½ teaspoon salt
3 cups sifted flour
1 cup powdered sugar
15–20 Popsicle sticks or short dowels
Colored icing (optional)
Favorite small candies (optional)

MIX butter and granulated sugar in a medium-sized mixing bowl; beat until light and fluffy. Add egg, milk or cream, and vanilla. Beat until smooth. Sift together baking soda, baking powder, salt, flour, and powdered sugar. Add dry ingredients slowly, mixing until well combined. (You may need to mix with your hands.) Form dough into a flattened ball, wrap in plastic wrap, and refrigerate for 45 minutes.

Preheat oven to 375°. Roll out the dough to a thickness of ¼" on a well-floured surface and cut out "flowers" with a round cookie cutter. Using an ungreased cookie sheet, place each "flower" on top of a Popsicle stick or short dowel, spacing the cookies at least 1" apart. Bake for 8 to 10 minutes. If desired, decorate with icing and favorite small candies.

MAKES 15 TO 20 FUN TREATS!

Posy Pots

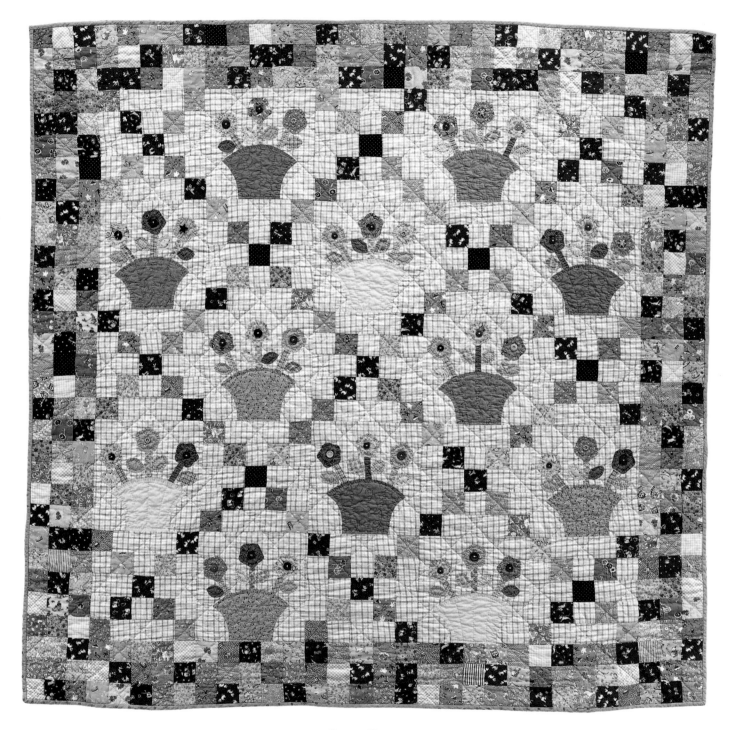

Posy Pots

by Nancy J. Martin, Woodinville, Washington, 2000. Quilted by Rose Schwartz, Hillsdale, Michigan.

Finished Quilt Size: 62" x 62"

Finished Block Size: 10" square

Materials

44"-wide fabric

- 3 fat quarters *each* of '30s prints in pink, blue, red, yellow, and green for blocks, appliqués, and border
- 2 yds. light plaid for appliqué background and blocks
- 1 fat eighth *each* of 2 different black prints for blocks and border
- 3¾ yds. fabric for backing
- 26" x 26" square of fabric for bias binding
- 66" x 66" square of lightweight batting
- 36 assorted buttons for flower centers

Cutting

All measurements include ¼"-wide seam allowances.

From *each* of the 3 pink, blue, red, yellow, and green fat quarters, cut:
- 27 squares, each 2½" x 2½", for blocks and border

From the light plaid, cut:
- 12 squares, each 11" x 11", for appliqué background
- 78 squares, each 2½" x 2½", for blocks
- 26 rectangles, 2½" x 4½", for blocks
- 26 rectangles, each 2½" x 6½", for blocks

From *each* fat eighth of black fabric, cut:
- 24 squares, each 2½" x 2½", for blocks and border

Note: *Refer to "Quiltmaking Basics" on pages 119–127 for guidance as needed with all basic quiltmaking techniques.*

Appliquéing the Posy Pot Blocks

You'll need 12 appliquéd Posy Pot blocks for this quilt.

1. Use the patterns on page 29 to make templates for appliqué pieces A–E. Trace the templates and cut 1 of piece C and 4 of piece D from each of the pink, blue, and yellow fat quarters; and 1 of piece C, 4 of piece A, 8 of piece B, and 16 of piece E from each of the green fat quarters.

2. Fold each 11" light plaid background square in half vertically, horizontally, and diagonally to find its center point; crease lightly. These guidelines will help you position the appliqués on the background squares.

3. Pin or baste the appliqués in place as shown. Use your preferred method to appliqué the stems, flowerpot, flowers, and leaves in alphabetical order to the background blocks. Trim each appliqué block to measure 10½" square.

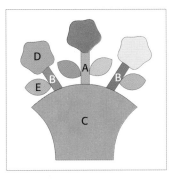

Appliqué Placement Diagram

Piecing the Irish Chain Blocks

You'll need 13 Irish Chain blocks for this quilt.

1. Arrange 8 assorted 2½" pink, blue, red, yellow, and green squares; six 2½" light plaid squares; 2 each of the 2½" x 4½" and 2½" x 6½" light plaid rectangles; and one 2½" black print square (in the center) to make a scrappy block as shown on page 28.

2. Sew the squares and strips together to make 5 rows as shown. Press seams away from the light plaid pieces.

3. Sew the rows together, pinning carefully to match the seams. Press seams as desired. Make 13 blocks.

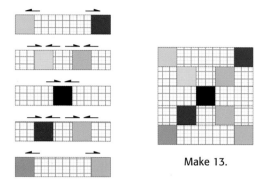

Make 13.

ASSEMBLING THE QUILT

1. Arrange alternating pieced and appliqué blocks in 5 horizontal rows of 5 blocks each. Odd-numbered rows begin with pieced blocks, while even-numbered rows begin with appliqué blocks.

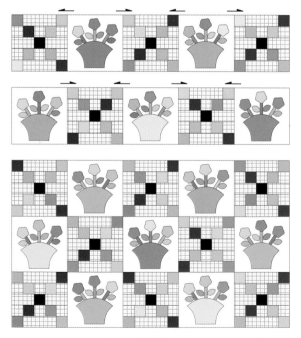

Assembly Diagram

2. Pin and sew the blocks together into rows. Press the seams toward the pieced blocks.

3. Carefully pin the rows together, matching the seams. Sew the rows together, and press seams in one direction.

MAKING AND ADDING THE BORDER

1. Refer to the color photo on page 26. Randomly arrange 25 remaining 2½" pink, blue, red, yellow, green, and black squares to make a horizontal row. Sew the squares together, and press seams to one side. Make 6 rows.

2. Carefully pin 2 rows together along their long edges, matching the seams. Sew the rows together, and press seams in one direction. Make 2 border units of 3 rows each.

3. Randomly arrange 31 remaining 2½" squares to make a horizontal row. Sew the squares together, and press seams to one side. Make 6 rows.

4. Repeat step 2 to make 2 border units of 3 rows each.

5. Sew a border unit from step 2 to opposite sides of the quilt. Press seams toward the border units. Sew a border unit from step 4 to the top and bottom of the quilt; press.

FINISHING

1. Mark the quilt top with the design of your choice. An overall diagonal grid helps unify the blocks.

2. Layer the quilt top with batting and backing; baste.

3. Hand or machine quilt as desired.

4. Trim the backing and batting even with the edges of the quilt top. Cut 2¼"-wide bias strips from the 26" square of binding fabric, for a total of approximately 260" of bias binding. Sew the binding to the quilt.

5. Securely stitch a button in the center of each flower.

6. Make and attach a label to your quilt.

Posy Pots
Appliqué Patterns

Appliqué patterns do not include seam allowance.

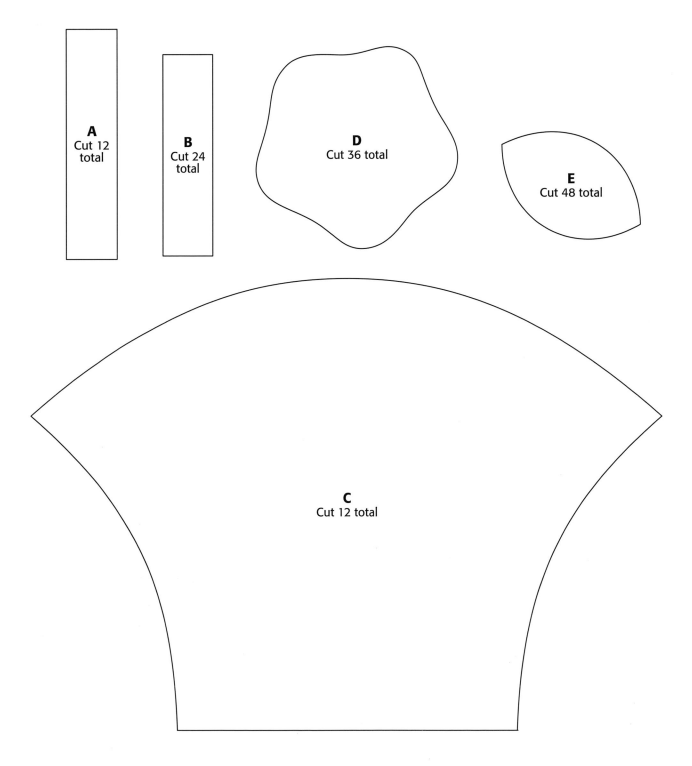

A
Cut 12 total

B
Cut 24 total

D
Cut 36 total

E
Cut 48 total

C
Cut 12 total

*H*FTER THE LONG, *gray winter months, the approach of summer signals the opportunity to escape everyday routines for new adventures. Sunrise reveals peaceful, greening meadows, while forests echo with the pleasing sounds of rain-fed streams, rustling leaves, and the sweet music of birdsong.*

Why not plan a special Father's Day picnic to help relieve the cabin fever of the long winter months? Take along this rustic flannel quilt, with its houndstooth patchwork and evergreen border, to comfort your tired fishermen after a day by the stream. Bring along "Grilled Meat with Rich and Savory Sauce" in case there are no fish to fry!

Grilled Meat with Rich and Savory Sauce

INGREDIENTS

1 medium carrot, finely diced
4 small shallots, chopped
1 clove garlic, chopped
2 tablespoons olive oil
2 or 3 bay leaves
1 tablespoon fresh thyme
2½ cups rich beef stock
1½ cups fresh Bing cherries, pitted and halved
⅓ cup balsamic vinegar
⅓ cup red wine
4 tablespoons unsalted butter, sliced
1 pound meat of choice (suggestions: pork tenderloin, lamb tenderloin, small beef ribeye steaks, pheasant breast)
salt and pepper to taste

IN a medium saucepan over medium-high heat, sauté carrots, shallots, and garlic in olive oil until slightly browned. Add bay leaves, thyme, and beef stock; bring to a boil. Reduce heat and simmer until liquid is reduced by half. Add cherries, vinegar, and wine. Cook until liquid has reduced by half again. Strain sauce into a bowl through a fine mesh strainer, and return liquid to pan. Add butter, stirring to thicken sauce. Allow to cool.

Salt and pepper meat to taste. Grill, and serve with sauce on top.

YIELD: ½ QUART; 4 TO 6 SERVINGS.

Cabin Fever

CABIN FEVER

by Suzette Halferty, Carnation, Washington, 2000. Quilted by Hattie Schrock, Millersburg, Ohio.

FINISHED QUILT SIZE: 60" x 60"

MATERIALS

44"-wide fabric

- 1 yd. green plaid for dark four-patch units and Tree blocks
- ¼ yd. burgundy print for dark four-patch units
- ¼ yd. black print for dark four-patch units
- ⅞ yd. light beige print for light four-patch units, triangle units, and corner squares
- ¼ yd. medium beige print #1 for light four-patch units
- 1½ yds. green print for triangle units and Tree blocks
- 1⅜ yds. medium beige print #2 for Tree blocks
- ⅜ yd. light green print for Tree blocks
- ⅛ yd. dark brown print for Tree blocks
- ⅜ yd. burgundy plaid for border
- ⅜ yd. black solid for corner appliqués
- 3¾ yds. fabric for backing
- 26" x 26" square of fabric for bias binding
- 64" x 64" square of lightweight batting
- ½ yd. lightweight fusible web
- Black embroidery floss

CUTTING

All measurements include ¼"-wide seam allowances. Use the patterns on page 37 to make templates for pieces A–E.

From the green plaid, cut:

- 32 squares, each 3½" x 3½", for dark four-patch units
- 16 regular and 16 reversed of piece D

From the burgundy print, cut:

- 16 squares, each 3½" x 3½", for dark four-patch units

From the black print, cut:

- 16 squares, each 3½" x 3½", for dark four-patch units

From the light beige print, cut:

- 18 squares, each 3½" x 3½", for light four-patch units
- 24 of piece A for triangle units
- 4 squares, each 9½" x 9½", for corner squares

From medium beige print #1, cut:

- 18 squares, each 3½" x 3½", for light four-patch units

From the green print, cut:

- 24 squares, each 5⅞" x 5⅞. Cut each square once diagonally to make 48 large triangles for triangle units.
- 32 squares, each 3⅛" x 3⅛". Cut each square once diagonally to make 64 small triangles for Tree blocks.
- 16 regular and 16 reversed of piece E

From medium beige print #2, cut:

- 16 regular and 16 reversed of piece B for Tree blocks
- 16 regular and 16 reversed of piece C for Tree blocks
- 16 squares, each 3⅛" x 3⅛". Cut each square once diagonally to make 32 triangles for Tree blocks.
- Cut 16 rectangles, each 1½" x 9½", for Tree blocks
- Cut 32 rectangles, 1¾" x 4½", for Tree blocks

From the light green print, cut:

- 16 squares, each 2⅜" x 2⅜". Cut each square once diagonally to make 32 small triangles for Tree blocks.
- 16 squares, each 3⅛" x 3⅛". Cut each square once diagonally to make 32 triangles for Tree blocks.

From the dark brown print, cut:

- 16 rectangles, each 1½" x 1¾", for Tree blocks

From the burgundy plaid, cut:

- 12 strips, each 2½" x 9½", for border

NOTE: *Refer to "Quiltmaking Basics" on pages 119–127 for guidance as needed with all basic quiltmaking techniques.*

Making the Quilt Center

You'll need 16 dark four-patch units, 9 light four-patch units, and 24 triangle units for this quilt. All units finish 6" square.

1. Arrange two 3½" green plaid squares, one 3½" burgundy-print square, and one 3½" black-print square to make a four-patch unit as shown. Sew the squares into rows; press seams toward the green squares. Pinning carefully to match seams, sew the rows together and press. Make 16 dark four-patch units.

Make 16.

2. Repeat step 1, using two 3½" light beige squares and two 3½" medium beige-print #1 squares to make a four-patch unit. Press seams toward the medium beige squares. Make 9 light four-patch units.

Make 9.

3. Arrange 1 of piece A between 2 large green-print triangles as shown. Sew the pieces together to make a triangle unit. Press seams toward the green triangles. Make 24.

Make 24.

4. Arrange 4 dark four-patch units and 3 triangle units to make a row as shown. Sew the units together; press seams toward the triangle units. Make 4 rows.

Make 4 rows.

5. Arrange 4 triangle units and 3 light four-patch units to make a row as shown. Sew the units together; press seams toward the triangle units. Make 3 rows.

Make 3 rows.

6. Beginning with a row from step 4, arrange alternating step 4 and step 5 rows as shown. Sew the rows together; press.

Assembly Diagram

Making and Attaching the Borders

You'll need 16 Tree blocks for the pieced border of this quilt. Each block finishes 9" square.

1. Sew a small green-print triangle to each regular piece B as shown in the block assembly diagram. Press seams toward the triangles. Make 16 units. Repeat to sew a small green-print triangle to each reversed piece B; press. Make 16 reversed units.

2. Sew a regular and reversed unit from step 1 together to make a row as shown. Press seams toward the regular unit. Make 16 rows.

3. Sew a small, light green-print triangle, a regular piece D, and a regular piece C in order shown. Press seams toward piece D. Make 16 units. Repeat to sew a small, light green-print triangle, a reversed piece D, and a reversed piece C in order shown; press. Make 16 reversed units.

4. Sew a regular and reversed unit from step 3 together to make a row as shown. Press seams toward the reverse unit. Make 16 rows.

5. Sew a large, light green-print triangle, a regular piece E, and a medium beige-print #2 triangle in order as shown. Press seams toward piece E. Make 16 units. Repeat to sew a large, light green-print triangle, a reversed piece E, and a medium beige-print #2 triangle in order shown; press. Make 16 reversed units.

6. Sew a regular and reversed unit from step 5 together to make a row as shown. Press seams toward the regular unit. Make 16 rows.

7. Sew one 1½" x 1¾" dark brown square between two 1¾" x 4½" medium beige-print #2 strips. Press seams toward the dark brown square. Make 16 rows.

8. Arrange a 1½" x 9½" medium beige-print #2 strip, and one row each from steps 2, 4, 6, and 7, as shown. Sew the rows together and press. Make 16.

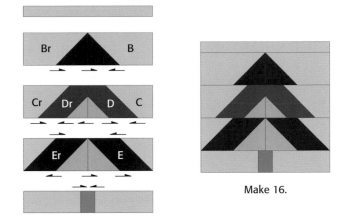

Block Assembly Diagram

Make 16.

9. Refer to the color photo on page 32. Arrange 4 Tree blocks and three 2½" x 9½" burgundy plaid strips to make a border unit as shown. Sew the blocks and strips together; press seams toward the strips. Make 4 border units.

10. Sew a border unit from step 9 to the top and bottom of the quilt, taking care to position the tree tops toward the quilt center as shown in the photo. Press seams toward the border units.

11. Refer to "Fusible-Web Appliqué" on page 120 and prepare the black solid fabric for fusing. Use the patterns on pages 36, 38, and 39 to make templates for appliqué pieces F–H. Use the templates to trace the following appliqués from the bonded fabric: 1 each of pieces F and G, and 2 of piece H.

12. Fold each 9½" light beige-print square twice diagonally to find its center point; crease lightly and unfold. Refer to the color photo on page 32. Turn each square on point, and follow the manufacturer's instructions to fuse one appliqué in the center of each square.

13. Use a buttonhole stitch and 3 strands of embroidery floss to secure the appliqués to the background squares.

14. Sew an appliquéd corner square to each end of a remaining border unit as shown. Press seams toward the corner squares.

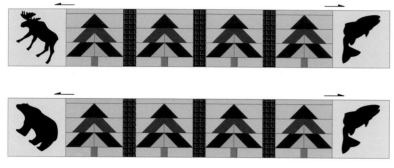

Make 1 of each.

15. Refer to the color photo on page 32. Sew a border unit from step 14 to opposite sides of the quilt, taking care to position the tree tops toward the quilt center. Press seams toward the border units.

FINISHING

1. Mark the quilt top with the design of your choice.

2. Layer quilt top with batting and backing; baste.

3. Hand or machine quilt as desired.

4. Trim the backing and batting even with the edges of the quilt top. Cut 2¼"-wide bias strips from the 26" square of binding fabric, for a total of approximately 250" of bias binding. Sew the binding to the quilt.

5. Make and attach a label to the quilt.

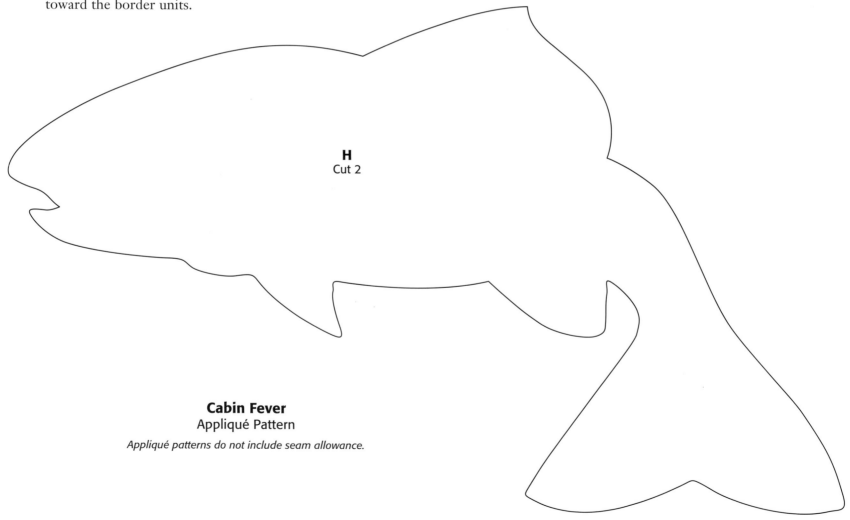

H
Cut 2

Cabin Fever
Appliqué Pattern

Appliqué patterns do not include seam allowance.

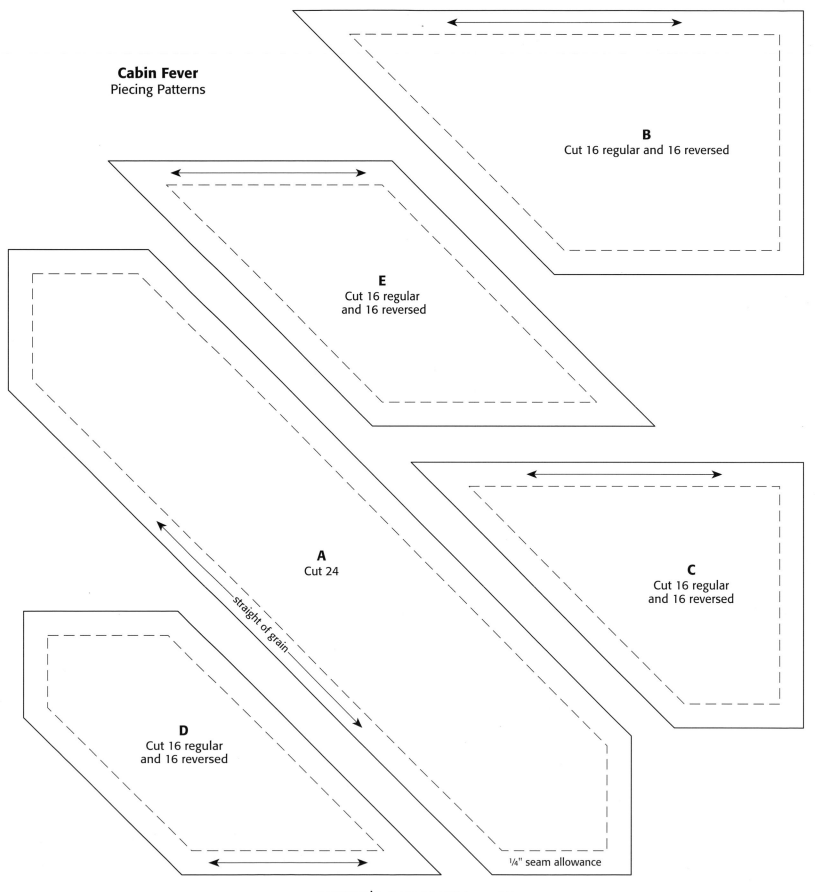

Cabin Fever
Piecing Patterns

B
Cut 16 regular and 16 reversed

E
Cut 16 regular
and 16 reversed

A
Cut 24

straight of grain

C
Cut 16 regular
and 16 reversed

D
Cut 16 regular
and 16 reversed

¼" seam allowance

Cabin Fever
Appliqué Pattern

Appliqué patterns do not include seam allowance.

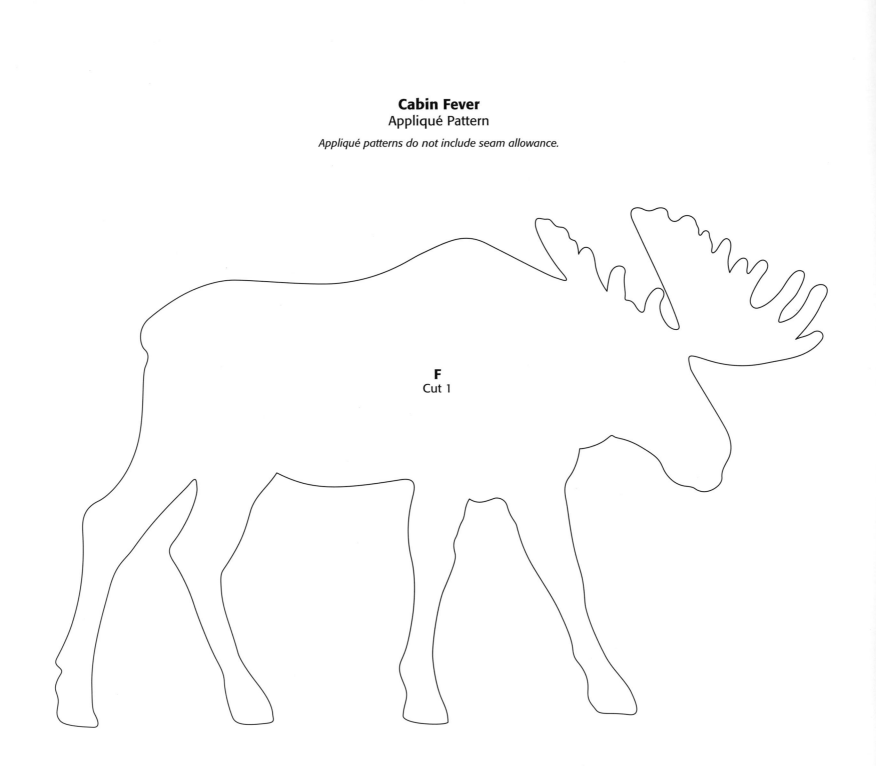

F
Cut 1

Cabin Fever
Appliqué Pattern

Appliqué patterns do not include seam allowance.

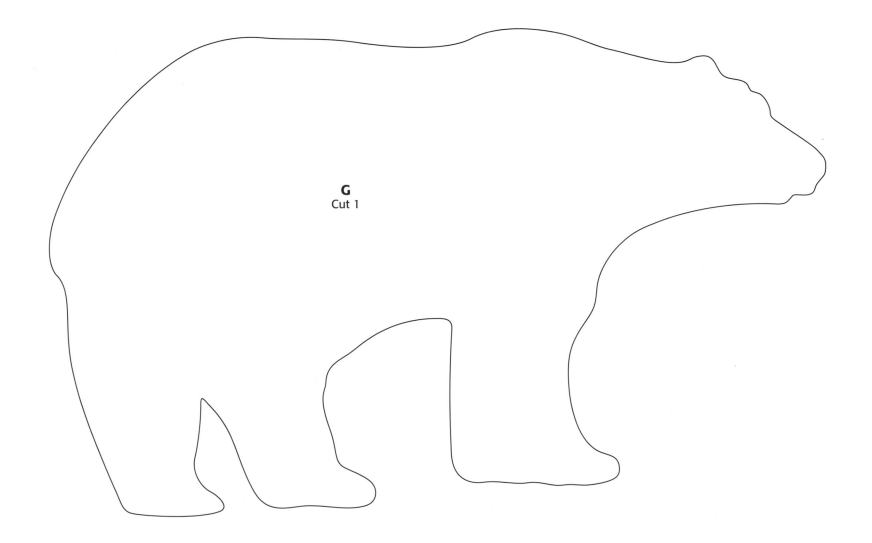

G
Cut 1

*B*LUE AND WHITE *is a color twosome we never seem to tire of, whether in our quilts or in our homes. We see this pleasing color combination repeatedly in fine china, wallpaper, and interior fabrics.*

Served on traditional Blue Willow dishes, a colorful summer fruit salad invites us to pause a moment and relax. It is hard to imagine a more refreshing dish to enhance a preconcert picnic in the park or alfresco lunch at a winery. Pack your dishes and a silverware carrier full of the necessary utensils in a wicker hamper to transport this elegant meal.

By selecting a sunny yellow fabric with the traditional Blue Willow motif, and combining it with various cool blue prints, we've given our summer-fresh "Blue Willow" quilt a wonderful, unexpected dimension. Once the fabrics are chosen, beginning and more experienced quilters alike will marvel at how quickly this quilt can be assembled.

Summer Fruit Salad

INGREDIENTS

2 cups white wine
½ cup orange juice
¼ cup honey
1 cinnamon stick
1 vanilla bean, split lengthwise
5 apricots, pitted and sliced
1 pound fresh blueberries

COMBINE the first 5 ingredients in a saucepan and bring to a boil. Reduce heat and simmer for 30 minutes. Scrape seeds from vanilla bean into the liquid; discard bean and cinnamon stick. Allow mixture to cool; then serve over fruit. May be prepared a day ahead and refrigerated. Delicious over pound cake!

YIELD: 4 TO 6 SERVINGS.

Blue Willow

BLUE WILLOW

by Nancy J. Martin, Woodinville, Washington, 2000. Quilted by Elizabeth Hostetler, Millersburg, Ohio.

FINISHED QUILT SIZE: 59¾" x 59¾"

FINISHED BLOCK SIZE: 16"

MATERIALS

44"-wide fabric

- ⅜ yd. *each* of 7 assorted blue prints on light backgrounds for blocks
- ½ yd. *each* of 7 assorted blue prints for blocks
- 1⅞ yds. large-scale, blue-and-yellow print for corner triangles and border*
- 26" x 26" square of fabric for bias binding
- 3¾ yds. fabric for backing
- 64" x 64" piece of lightweight batting

* Yardage is based on cutting the large triangles along the straight grain of the fabric. If you have a theme print you would like to cut so that the print in all the triangles appears right side up, purchase an additional half-yard of fabric.

CUTTING

All measurements include ¼"-wide seam allowances.

From *each* of the 7 blue prints on light backgrounds, cut:
- 13 squares (91 total), each 2⅞" x 2⅞". Cut each square once diagonally to make 182 triangles for blocks. You'll have 6 triangles left over.
- 2 squares (14 total), each 8" x 8", for bias squares

From *each* of the 7 blue prints, cut:
- 4 squares (28 total), each 5¼" x 5¼". Cut each square twice diagonally to make 112 large triangles for blocks. You'll have 4 triangles left over.
- 2 squares (14 total), each 8" x 8", for bias squares
- 3 squares (21 total), each 4" x 4". Cut each square twice diagonally to make 84 small triangles. You'll have 4 triangles left over.
- 4 squares (28 total), each 2½" x 2½", for blocks. You'll have 4 squares left over.

- 1 square (7 total), each 3⅜" x 3⅜". You'll have 3 squares left over.

From *one* of the blue prints, cut:
- 1 square, 4" x 4", for center of Block B

From the large-scale, blue-and-yellow print, cut:
- 8 squares, each 8⅞" x 8⅞". Cut each square once diagonally to make 16 corner triangles.*
- 6 strips, each 7¼" x 44", for border

* If using fabric that requires special cutting to make the print appear right side up in each triangle, cut 4 squares, each 12½" x 12½". Cut each square twice diagonally to make 16 triangles. Be careful not to stretch the long bias edges.

NOTE: *Refer to "Quiltmaking Basics" on pages 119–127 for guidance as needed with all basic quiltmaking techniques.*

MAKING THE BLOCKS

YOU'LL NEED to make 4 of Block A, 1 of Block B, 4 half blocks, and 4 quarter blocks for this quilt. Make the blocks as scrappy as you wish.

Block A

1. Sew a triangle cut from a blue print with a light background to each side of a 3⅜" blue square. Press seams toward triangles. Make 4.

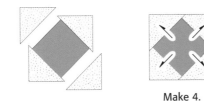

Make 4.

2. Sew a triangle cut from a blue print with a light background to each short side of a large blue-print triangle to make a Flying Geese unit. Press seams toward light triangles. Make 80. Set 48 aside for now.

Make 80.

3. Pair each 8" square cut from a blue print with a light background with an 8" blue-print square, right sides up. Cut and piece 2½"-wide bias strips (see page 119). Cut 112 bias squares, each 2½" x 2½".

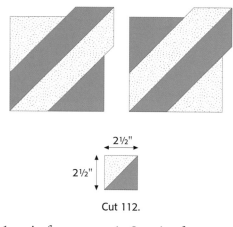

Cut 112.

4. Arrange 1 unit from step 1, 8 units from step 2, 4 bias squares from step 3, 4 large blue-print triangles, and 8 small blue-print triangles as shown. Pin and then sew the units, bias squares, and triangles together to make 3 "rows." Press seams in opposite directions from row to row.

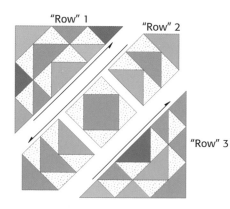

5. Carefully pin the rows, matching the seams. Sew the rows together and press. Finish the block by sewing a large-scale, blue-and-yellow triangle on each corner. Press seams toward the corner triangles. Make a total of 4 blocks, and label them Block A.

Block A
Make 4.

Block B

1. Arrange three 2½" blue-print squares and 6 bias squares (Block A, step 3) in 3 rows, taking care to position the bias squares as shown below. Sew the blue-print squares and bias squares into rows; press seams in opposite directions from row to row.

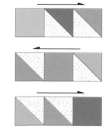

2. Carefully pin the rows, matching the seams. Sew the rows together and press. Make 8. Set 4 aside for now.

3. Sew 3 Flying Geese units (page 43, step 2) in a vertical row; press seams in one direction. Make 4.

Make 4.

4. Arrange the 4" blue-print square, 4 units from step 2, and units from step 3, in 3 rows. Take care to position the units as shown. Sew the units and 4" square into rows; press seams in opposite directions from row to row.

5. Carefully pin the rows, matching the seams. Sew the rows together and press. Make 1, and label it Block B.

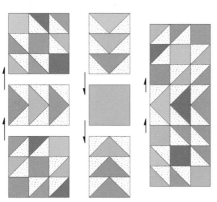

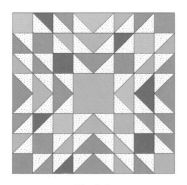

Block B
Make 1.

Half and Quarter Blocks

1. Arrange 3 bias squares (page 44, step 3) and 3 small blue-print triangles as shown. Sew the bias squares and triangles into rows; press seams in opposite directions from row to row.

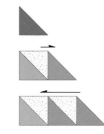

2. Carefully pin the rows, matching the seams. Sew the rows together and press. Make 16 triangle units.

3. Sew 3 Flying Geese units (page 43, step 2) in a vertical row as shown; press seams in one direction. Make 12.

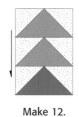

Make 12.

4. Sew 2 large blue-print triangles to a triangle unit from step and a Flying Geese unit from step 3 as shown; press.

5. Sew a triangle unit from step 2, a Flying Geese unit from step 3, and a remaining Block B (pages 44 and 45, steps 1 and 2) unit together as shown. Press.

6. Sew units from steps 4 and 5 together as shown; press. Repeat steps 1–5 to make 4 half blocks.

Half Block
Make 4.

7. Arrange 2 triangle units from step 2, a large blue-print triangle, and 1 Flying Geese unit from step 3, taking care to position the units as shown. Sew the units together, and press seams in one direction. Make 4 and label them Quarter blocks.

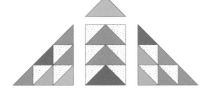 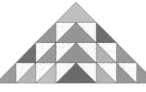

Quarter Block
Make 4.

ASSEMBLING THE QUILT

1. Arrange A and B Blocks, Half blocks, and Quarter blocks in diagonal rows as shown.

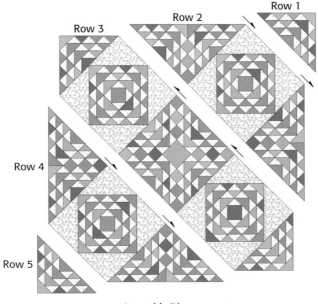

Assembly Diagram

2. Pin and then sew the A, B, Half, and Quarter blocks to make 5 diagonal rows. Press seams in opposite directions from row to row.

3. Carefully pin the rows, matching the seams. Sew the rows together, and press.

4. Divide two 7¼" x 44" border strips in half, and sew one half to each remaining 7¼" x 44" border strip.

5. Measure the quilt through its vertical center, and trim 2 borders to that measurement. Sew a trimmed border strip to opposite sides of the quilt. Press seams toward the border strips.

6. Measure the quilt through its horizontal center and trim the remaining 2 borders to that measurement. Sew a trimmed border to the top and bottom of the quilt; press.

FINISHING

1. Mark the quilt top with a design of your choice.

2. Layer the quilt top with batting and backing; baste.

3. Hand or machine quilt as desired.

4. Trim the backing and batting even with the edges of the quilt top. Cut 2¼"-wide bias strips from the 26" square of binding fabric, for a total of approximately 250" of bias binding. Sew the binding to the quilt.

5. Make and attach a label to your quilt.

Companion Project: Silverware Carrier

MATERIALS

44"-wide fabric

- ⅜ yd. quilted fabric (you may quilt two of your favorite fabrics together)
- ⅜ yd. fabric for silverware pockets and tie
- ¼ yd. matching or contrasting fabric for bias binding

CUTTING

All measurements include ¼"-wide seam allowances.

From the quilted fabric, cut:
- 1 piece, 12" x 34", for silverware carrier

From the pocket and tie fabric, cut:
- 1 piece, 12" x 34", for pockets
- 1 strip, 2" x 44", for ties

ASSEMBLY

1. With right sides out, fold the pocket fabric in half to form a 6" x 34" strip for the silverware pockets; press.

2. Press a crease down the center of the 2" x 44" fabric strip. Open the fabric so that it is flat with wrong side up. Fold the raw edges over to meet at the crease line; press. Fold in half along the original crease line; press. Stitch close to the folded edges.

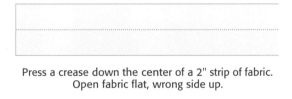

Press a crease down the center of a 2" strip of fabric.
Open fabric flat, wrong side up.

Fold raw edges over to the crease line; press.

Fold in half along original crease line; press.
Stitch close to folded edges.

SILVERWARE CARRIER
by Nancy J. Martin, Woodinville, Washington, 2000.

Cut in half to make 2 ties. With right side of quilted fabric facing up, pin ties to center of one short side.

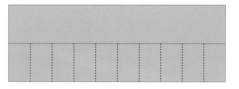

3. With right sides facing and raw edges even, lay the pocket strip on top of the quilted fabric. Pin in place and baste around all sides.

4. Divide the pocket strip into the desired number of sections and mark. Stitch a straight line from the top of the pocket to the bottom.

5. Use the matching or contrasting fabric to cut and piece 2¼"-wide bias strips to make 96" of bias binding. Bind edges of the carrier with bias strips.

6. Fill pockets with silverware, roll to close, and tie with the doublefold strip.

B Y INDEPENDENCE DAY, *summer has truly arrived. After a pleasant day of parades, swimming, boating, and friendly ballgames in the park, celebrate the summer holiday at a barbeque picnic with all the trimmings, including fresh tomatoes, berry pies, and homemade ice cream.*

Our snappy quilt "Stars and Stripes" echoes the patriotic tone of our most historic holiday and is perfect for enjoying a burst of evening fireworks. Its feathered star medallion, surrounded by an explosion of crisp appliquéd stars, is certain to bring back fond memories of summer's gatherings all year long.

Fresh Tomato Tart

INGREDIENTS FOR TART SHELL

1 ½ cups all-purpose flour
6 tablespoons frozen butter, cut into small pieces
½ teaspoon salt
1 egg plus 1 egg yolk
1 tablespoon plus 1 teaspoon lemon juice

INGREDIENTS FOR TART

10" tart shell (see ingredients above)
3 tablespoons Dijon mustard
½ pound Gruyère cheese, grated
¼ cup fresh basil, snipped
6 ripe tomatoes, sliced about ¼" thick
3 tablespoons brown sugar
Fresh basil for garnish

PREHEAT oven to 425°. To make tart shell, combine flour, butter, and salt in a food processor with a metal blade. Process in short bursts until pea-size clumps form (about 10 seconds). Drizzle eggs and lemon juice through food chute, with machine running, until a ball of dough forms on blade. (If dough seems too soft, sprinkle with 1 to 2 tablespoons of flour and combine.)

Turn dough onto plastic wrap, form into a flat disk, and refrigerate for 30 minutes.

On a floured surface, roll chilled dough into a circle large enough for a 10" tart pan. Press dough into pan and bake for 10 minutes. Allow to cool slightly.

Brush the cooled shell with Dijon mustard. Sprinkle with grated cheese and snipped basil, top with sliced tomatoes, and sprinkle with brown sugar. Bake 10 to 15 minutes, until the cheese melts and the tomatoes become tender. Place a sprig of fresh basil in the center for garnish.

YIELD: 6 SERVINGS.

Stars and Stripes

STARS AND STRIPES

by Nancy J. Martin, Woodinville, Washington, 1999. Quilted by Alvina Nelson, Salina, Kansas.

Finished Quilt Size: 60" x 60"

Materials

44"-wide fabric

- ¾ yd. blue print on light background for Feathered Star block, pieced border, and star appliqués
- 1½ yds. red print for Feathered Star block, first and second accent borders, and bias binding
- 2 yds. large-scale blue print for Feathered Star block and outer border
- ⅞ yd. cream-on-cream print for pieced border
- ¾ yd. small-scale blue print for pieced border
- ¾ yd. red-and-white striped fabric for pieced border
- 3¾ yds. fabric for backing
- 64" x 64" piece of lightweight batting

Cutting

All measurements include ¼"-wide seam allowances. Use the patterns on pages 56–58 to make templates for pieces A–D.

From the blue print on a light background, cut:
- 1 piece, 11" x 18", for bias squares
- 1 square, 11¼" x 11¼". Cut twice diagonally to make 4 large triangles for Feathered Star block triangle units.
- 4 squares, each 2" x 2". Cut each square once diagonally to make 8 triangles for Feathered Star block triangle units.
- 4 squares, each 6" x 6", for Feathered Star block corner square units
- 4 squares, each 1⅞" x 1⅞". Cut each square once diagonally to make 8 triangles for Feathered Star block corner square units.

From the red print, cut:
- 2 strips, each 2" x 21½", along the *lengthwise* grain for first accent border
- 2 strips, each 2" x 24½", along the *lengthwise* grain for first accent border

- 2 strips, each 2½" x 44½", along the *lengthwise* grain for second accent border
- 2 strips, each 2½" x 48½", along the *lengthwise* grain for second accent border
- 1 piece, 11" x 18", for bias squares
- 4 regular and 4 reversed of piece A
- 26" x 26" square for bias binding

From the large-scale blue print, cut:
- 2 strips, each 6¼"x 48½", along the *lengthwise* grain for outer border
- 2 strips, each 6¼" x 60", along the *lengthwise* grain for outer border
- 4 squares, each 4⅞" x 4⅞". Cut each square once diagonally to make 8 triangles for Feathered Star block points.
- 1 square, 8½" x 8½", for Feathered Star block center

From the cream-on-cream print, cut:
- 26 squares, each 4⅞" x 4⅞". Cut each square once diagonally to make 52 triangles for pieced border.
- 4 regular and 4 reversed of piece D

From the small-scale blue print, cut:
- 6 regular and 6 reversed of piece B
- 2 regular and 2 reversed of piece C

From the red-and-white striped fabric, cut:
- 6 regular and 6 reversed of piece B. Take care to align stripe as marked on pattern.
- 2 regular and 2 reversed of piece C. Take care to align stripe as marked on pattern.

Note: *Refer to "Quiltmaking Basics" on pages 119–127 for guidance as needed with all basic quiltmaking techniques.*

PIECING THE FEATHERED STAR BLOCK

THERE ARE 2 sizes of bias squares cut for this Feathered Star block: 1½" and 1⅝". Keep the different-size units in separate, labeled, resealable bags. The 1½" bias squares are used to construct the corner square units. The 1⅝" bias squares are used in constructing the triangle units.

1. Pair the 11" x 18" piece of red print with the 11" x 18" piece of blue print on light background, right sides up. Cut and piece 1¾"-wide bias strips (see page 119). *Be sure to press seams open and flat.* Cut 36 bias squares, each 1⅝" x 1⅝", and 28 bias squares, each 1½" x 1½".

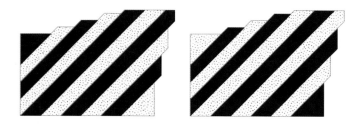

2. Sew a 2" triangle cut from the blue print with light background and four 1⅝" bias squares from step 1 into a row, taking care to position the pieces as shown. Press seams to one side. Make 4.

Make 4.

3. Sew a 2" triangle cut from the blue print with light background and five 1⅝" bias squares from step 1 into a row; press. Make 4.

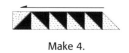

Make 4.

NOTE: *You will be sewing partial seams when piecing the triangle units in steps 4–6. The seams are completed as the block is assembled.*

4. Stitch a unit from step 2 to the short left side of each large triangle cut from the blue print with the light background, sewing a partial seam as shown. Press seams toward the large triangle. Make 4.

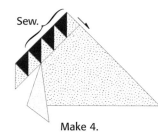

Make 4.

5. Repeat to sew a unit from step 3 to the short right side of each unit from step 4; press.

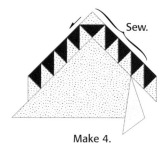

Make 4.

6. Sew a large-scale blue-print triangle to both short sides of each unit from step 5. Press seams toward the blue-print triangles. Make 4.

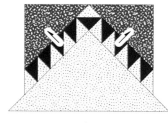

Make 4.

7. Sew a piece A, a 1⅞" triangle cut from the blue print with light background, and three 1½" bias squares into a row, taking care to position the pieces as shown. Align the notch of piece A with the long edge of the 1⅞" triangle. Press seams to one side. Make 4.

8. Sew a reversed piece A, a 1⅞" triangle cut from the blue print with light background, and four 1½" bias squares into a row; press. Be sure to align the marked edge on reversed piece A with the long edge of the 1⅞"triangle. Make 4.

Make 4.

9. Sew a unit from step 7 to the top edge of each 6" square cut from the blue print with light background, taking care to position the unit as shown. Press seams toward the 6" square. Make 4.

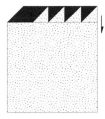

Make 4.

10. Repeat to sew a unit from step 8 to the right edge of each unit from step 9; press. Make 4.

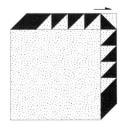

Make 4.

11. Sew a triangle unit from step 6 between 2 corner square units from step 10. Finish sewing the partial seams. Press seams toward the triangle unit. Make 2.

Finish sewing partial seams.

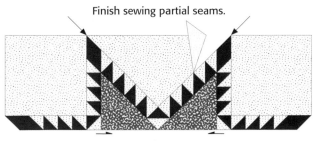

Make 2.

12. Sew the 8½" large-scale blue-print square between the 2 remaining triangle units from step 6 as shown in the block assembly diagram below. Press seams toward the triangle units.

13. Sew the row from step 12 between the 2 rows from step 11 as shown in the block assembly diagram. Finish sewing the partial seams; press.

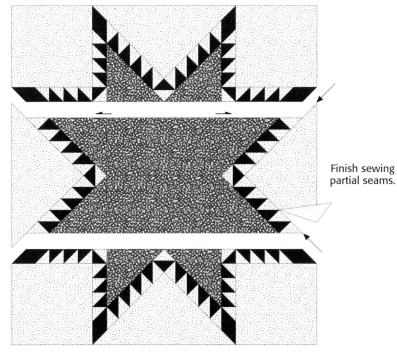

Finish sewing partial seams.

Block Assembly Diagram

MAKING AND ADDING THE BORDERS

1. Sew a red 2" x 21½" first accent border strip to opposite sides of the Feathered Star block. Press seams toward the border strips. Sew a red 2" x 24½" first accent border strip to the top and bottom of the block; press.

2. Sew a cream-print triangle to both diagonal notched edges of each blue regular and reversed piece B. Press seams toward each piece B. Make 6 of each.

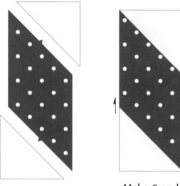

Make 6 and
6 reversed.

3. Sew 2 cream-print triangles to both notched edges of each red-and-white striped regular and reversed B piece; press. Make 6 of each.

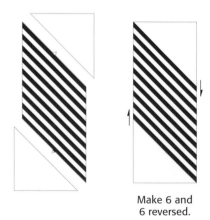

Make 6 and
6 reversed.

4. Use the patterns on pages 56 and 58 to make templates for appliqué pieces E and F. Trace the templates and cut 12 of piece E and 2 of piece F from scraps of the blue print with light background.

5. Refer to the color photo on page 50. Pin or baste a small star appliqué (piece E) to each unit from step 2, centering it on the blue piece B as shown. Use your preferred method to appliqué the stars in place.

6. Arrange 3 red-and-white striped regular B units from step 3 and 3 blue reversed B units from step 5 to make a border unit as shown. Sew the units together, and press to one side. Make 2.

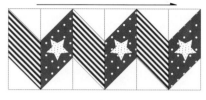

Make 2.

7. Repeat to sew 3 red-and-white striped reversed B units to 3 blue regular B units to make 2 border units; press.

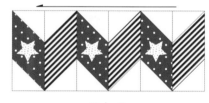

Make 2.

8. Refer to the color photo on page 50. Sew a border unit from step 7 to opposite sides of the quilt, making sure to position it as shown. Press seams toward the first accent border.

9. Sew a cream regular D piece and a red-and-white striped regular C piece as shown. Press seams toward piece C. Make 2.

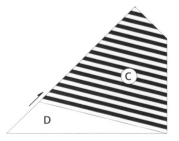

Make 2.

10. Sew a cream reversed D piece and a red-and-white striped reversed C piece; press. Make 2.

11. Sew a unit from step 9, a unit from step 10, and a cream-print triangle to make a new unit as shown; press. Make 2.

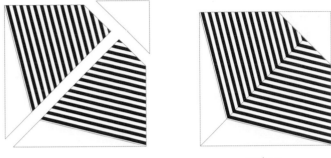

Make 2.

12. Repeat steps 9 through 11 to sew 2 units as shown. Substitute the small-scale, blue-print regular and reversed C pieces for the red-and-white striped C pieces. Make 2.

Make 2.

13. Sew a unit from step 11 and step 12 to each end of a border unit from step 6 as shown. Press seams toward the corner units.

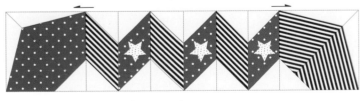

Make 2.

14. Sew a border unit from step 13 to the top and bottom of the quilt. Refer to the color photo on page 50 for guidance as needed. Press seams toward the accent border.

15. Use your preferred method to appliqué a large star appliqué (F) over the center seam in each unit from step 12.

16. Sew a red 2½" x 44½" second accent border strip to opposite sides of the quilt top. Press seams toward the second accent border. Sew a 2½" x 48½" second accent border strip to the top and bottom of the quilt; press. Sew the blue 6¼" x 48½" outer border strips to the sides, and the blue 6¼" x 60" outer border strips to the top and bottom of the quilt; press.

FINISHING

1. Mark the quilt top with a design of your choice.

2. Layer the quilt top with batting and backing; baste.

3. Hand or machine quilt as desired.

4. Trim the backing and batting even with the edges of the quilt top. Cut 2¼"-wide bias strips from the 26" square of binding fabric, for a total of approximately 250" of bias binding. Sew the binding to the quilt.

5. Make and attach a label to your quilt.

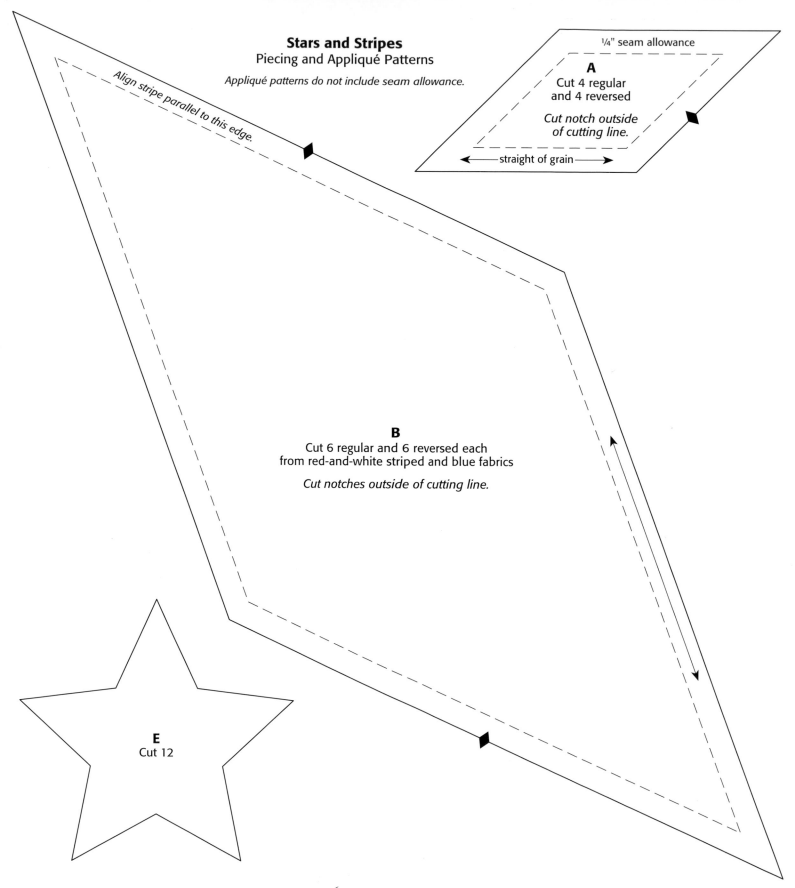

Stars and Stripes
Piecing and Appliqué Patterns

Appliqué patterns do not include seam allowance.

¼" seam allowance

A
Cut 4 regular
and 4 reversed

*Cut notch outside
of cutting line.*

← straight of grain →

Align stripe parallel to this edge.

B
Cut 6 regular and 6 reversed each
from red-and-white striped and blue fabrics

Cut notches outside of cutting line.

E
Cut 12

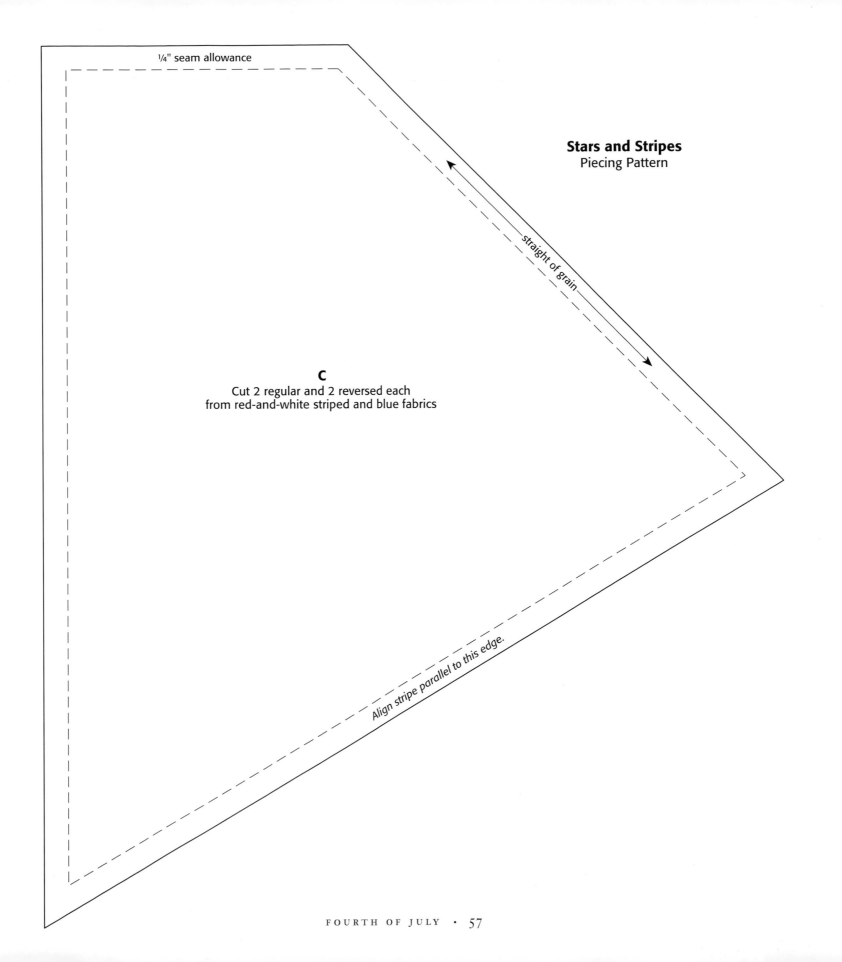

¼" seam allowance

Stars and Stripes
Piecing Pattern

straight of grain

C
Cut 2 regular and 2 reversed each
from red-and-white striped and blue fabrics

Align stripe parallel to this edge.

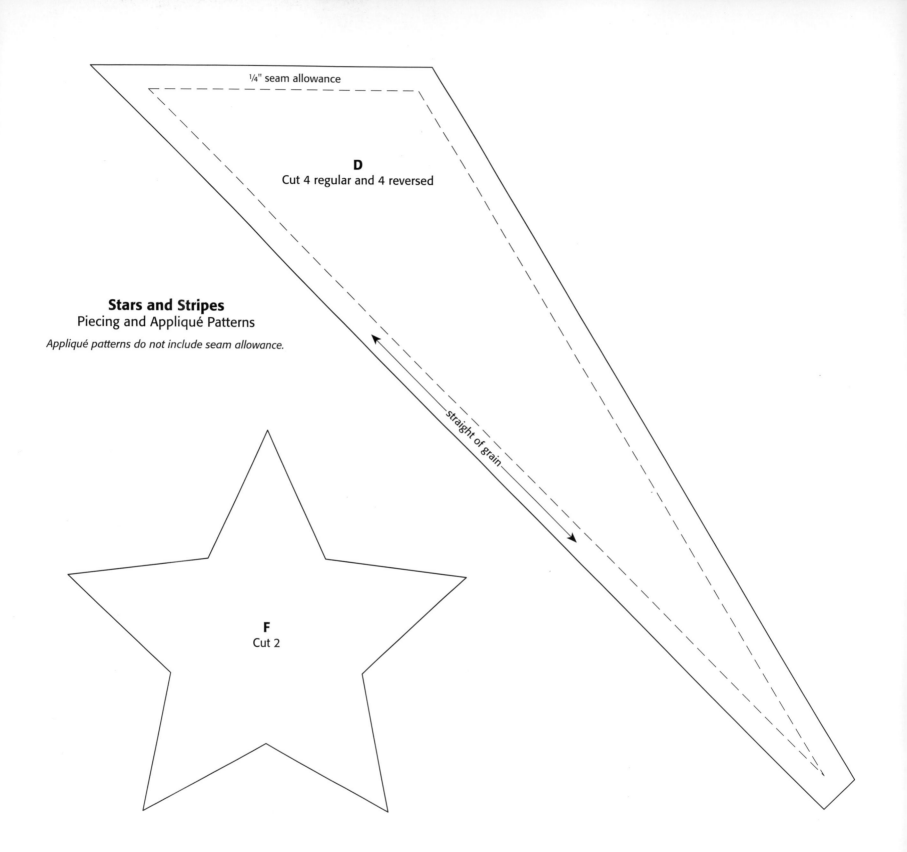

¼" seam allowance

D
Cut 4 regular and 4 reversed

Stars and Stripes
Piecing and Appliqué Patterns

Appliqué patterns do not include seam allowance.

straight of grain

F
Cut 2

Companion Project: Casserole Carrier

Finished Size: 15" x 19" *(holds 2-quart casserole dish)*

Materials

44"-wide fabric

- 1 yd. quilted fabric (you may quilt 2 of your favorite fabrics together)
- ⅜ yd. contrasting fabric for bias binding
- ⅜ yd. red-striped fabric for handles and casing
- ⅛ yd. white fabric for appliqué stars
- Black embroidery floss
- 1½ yds. ribbon for drawstring

Cutting

All measurements include ¼"-wide seam allowances. See page 56 for piece E (star appliqué).

From the quilted fabric, cut:
- 2 pieces, each 16" x 20", for carrier bottom and carrier top
- 2 strips, each 2½" x 22", for handles

From the red-striped fabric, cut:
- 2 strips, each 2½" x 22", for handles
- 1 bias strip, 2¾" x 26", for drawstring casing*

From the white fabric, cut:
- 5 of piece E for appliqué. *Do not add seam allowance.*

*Refer to page 125 for guidance in cutting bias strips.

Assembly

1. Fold each 16" x 20" piece of quilted fabric into fourths. Use the pattern pieces on pages 60–61 to cut 1 carrier top and 1 carrier bottom.

2. Cut 2¼"-wide bias strips from the contrasting fabric to make approximately 5½ yards (188") of bias binding.

CASEROLE CARRIER
by Cleo Nollette, Seattle, Washington, 2000.

3. Pair a 2½" x 22" quilted handle strip and a 2½" x 22" red-striped handle strip, wrong (lining) sides together. Use the binding from step 2 to bind the long edges of the handle strip. Make and bind 2 handles.

4. Use 2 strands of black embroidery floss and a buttonhole stitch to embroider and appliqué the 5 stars to the carrier top.

5. Cut two 2¼" x 8" bias strips from remaining scrap of lining fabric. Use the strips to bind the short, straight edges of the carrier top.

6. Fold over and stitch the short raw edges of the 2¾" x 26" red-striped bias strip. Use this strip to bind the inner curved edges of the carrier top. Leave the finished ends open to create a casing. Insert ribbon in casing to form a drawstring.

7. Pin carrier top to carrier bottom, wrong (lining) sides together. Pin the handles in place as shown. Baste the outer edges together all around the perimeter of the carrier. Be sure to stitch through all layers, including handle ends.

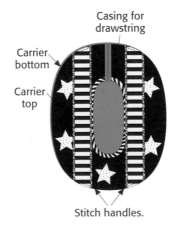

8. Use the remaining binding from step 2 to bind the outer edges of the carrier.

9. Insert casserole in carrier, and pull drawstrings to close. Tie drawstrings in a bow.

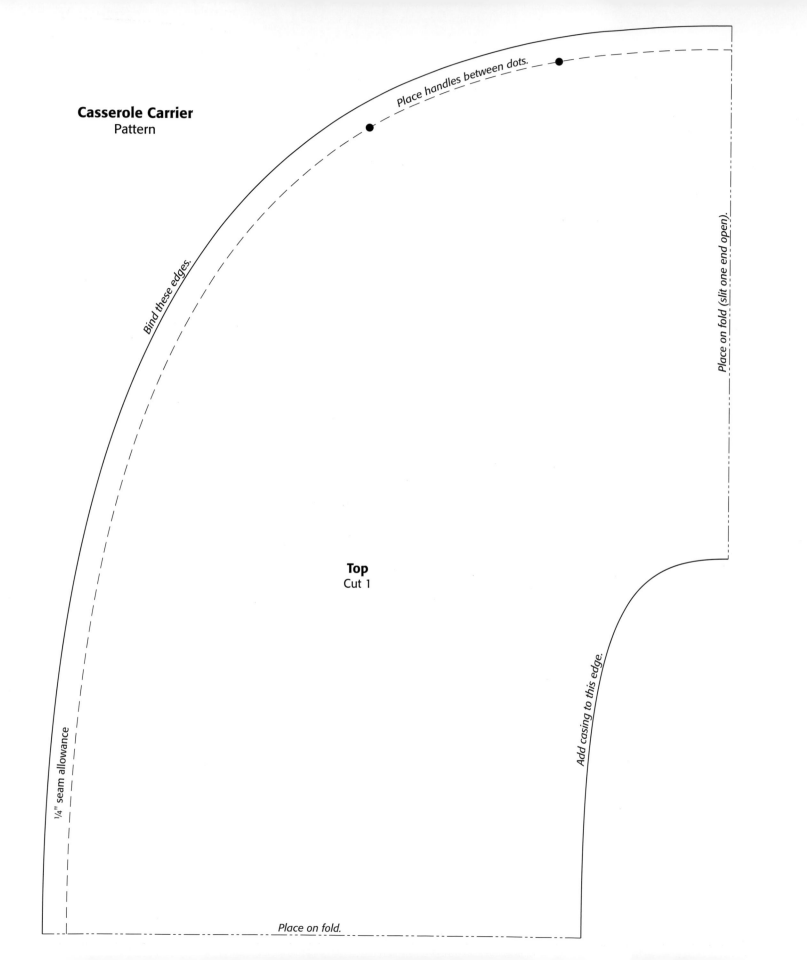

Casserole Carrier
Pattern

Place handles between dots.

Bind these edges.

Place on fold (slit one end open).

Top
Cut 1

Add casing to this edge.

¼" seam allowance

Place on fold.

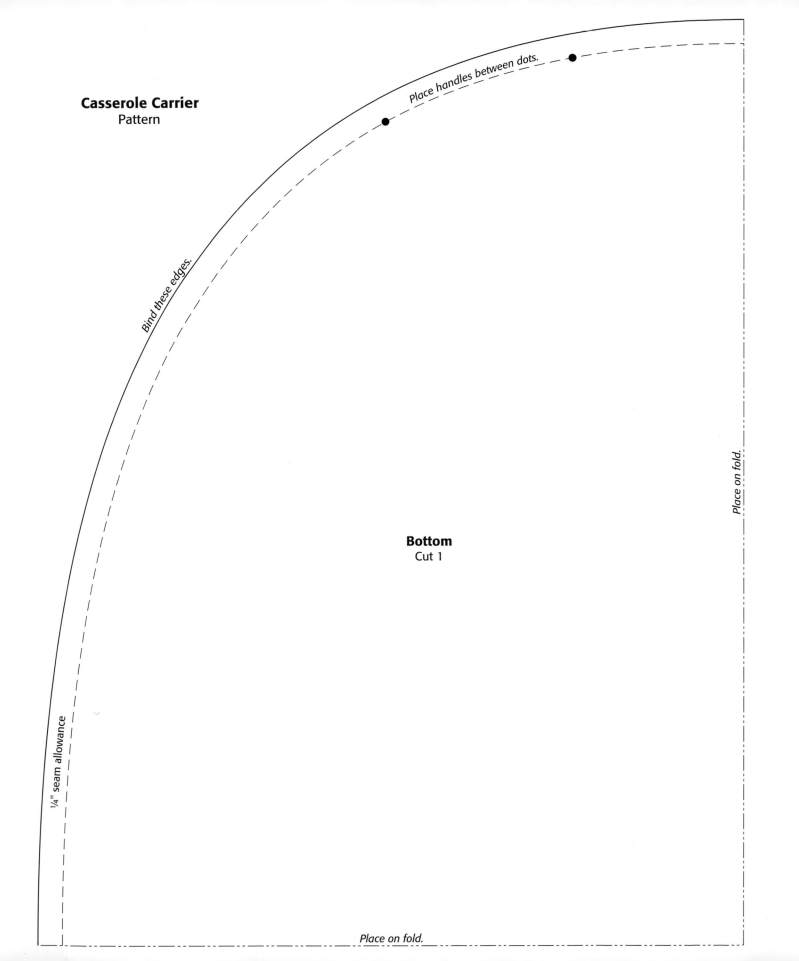

Casserole Carrier
Pattern

Place handles between dots.

Bind these edges.

Place on fold.

Bottom
Cut 1

¼" seam allowance

Place on fold.

P ASSING THE LONG *hazy days of summer at the seashore is a cherished tradition in many parts of the country, creating the opportunity for lasting family memories. Whether your chosen spot is beside a sailboat-dotted harbor or on a quiet stretch of beach, a picnic becomes a special occasion when celebrated where the sky meets the sea.*

For a beach picnic or dinner on the dock, serve Sand Dune Salad and show off our gay sailboat quilt. Nine easy-to-appliqué sailboats skim along the blue waves, helping recall happy seaside days for many years to come.

Sand Dune Salad

INGREDIENTS

⅓ pound scallops, grilled

⅓ pound prawns (approximately 12), peeled and grilled

4 ears corn, cooked and cut from cob (approximately 2 cups)

2 cups red cherry tomatoes, sliced in half

1 roasted red pepper, skin removed and sliced

2 tablespoons fresh cilantro, finely chopped

¼ cup olive oil

2 tablespoons red wine vinegar or balsamic vinegar

½ teaspoon salt

COMBINE seafood, corn, tomatoes, and red pepper in a bowl. In a separate bowl mix cilantro, oil, vinegar, and salt. Pour over seafood and vegetable mixture, and stir until combined. This delicious picnic salad can be made ahead of time, and easily transported in a resealable plastic bag. If you do make the salad ahead, add the grilled seafood just prior to serving.

YIELD: 4 SERVINGS.

Seashore Dreamin'

SEASHORE DREAMIN'
by Suzette Halferty and That Patchwork Place staff, Carnation and Woodinville, Washington, 2000. Quilted by Frankie Schmidt, Bothell, Washington.

Finished Quilt Size: 63" x 63"

Materials

44"-wide fabric

- 1 yd. white solid for sail appliqués
- ¼ yd. bright red solid for sail trim appliqués
- ⅛ yd. striped fabric for flag appliqués
- ⅛ yd. navy solid for mast appliqués
- ⅜ yd. dark red solid or subtle print for sailboat hull appliqués
- 3½ yds. medium blue print for background and outer border
- 1 fat quarter dark blue solid for waves
- ½ yd. striped fabric for inner border
- 3¾ yds. fabric for backing
- 26" x 26" square of fabric for bias binding
- 67" x 67" square of lightweight batting

Cutting

All measurements include ¼"-wide seam allowances.

From the medium blue print, cut:

- 9 squares, each 13" x 13", for appliqué background
- 1 piece, 11" x 15", for bias squares
- 9 strips, each 6½" x 10½", for half blocks
- 9 strips, each 1½" x 6½", for half blocks
- 4 strips, each 5" x 54½", along the *lengthwise* grain for sashing
- 2 strips, each 3¼" x 63", along the *lengthwise* grain for outer border
- 2 strips, each 3¼" x 57½", along the *lengthwise* grain for outer border

From the dark blue solid, cut:

- 1 piece, 11" x 15", for bias squares

From the striped fabric for inner border, cut:

- 6 strips, each 2" x 44", for inner border

Note: *Refer to "Quiltmaking Basics" on pages 119–127 for guidance as needed with all basic quiltmaking techniques.*

Appliquéing the Blocks

You'll need 9 Sailboat blocks for this quilt.

1. Use the patterns on pages 67–69 to make templates for appliqué pieces A–F. Trace the templates and cut 9 each of pieces A and B from the white solid, 9 of piece C from the bright red solid, 9 of piece D from the ⅛ yard striped fabric for flag appliqués, 9 of piece E from the navy solid, and 9 of piece F from the dark red solid or subtle print.

2. Fold each 13" medium blue print square in half vertically, horizontally, and diagonally to find its center point; crease lightly. These guidelines will help you position the appliqués on the background squares.

3. Pin or baste the appliqués in place as shown. Use your preferred method to appliqué the sails, trim, flag, mast, and hull in alphabetical order to each background block. Trim each appliqué block to measure 12½" square.

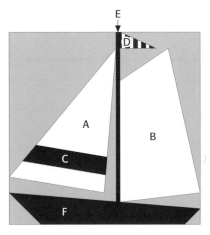

Appliqué Placement Diagram

Piecing the Half Blocks

You'll need 9 half blocks for this quilt.

1. Pair the 11" x 15" piece of medium blue print with the 11" x 15" piece of dark blue solid, right sides up. Cut and piece 1¾"-wide bias strips (see page 119). *Be sure to press seams open and flat.* Cut 54 bias squares, each 1½" x 1½".

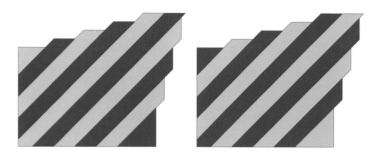

2. Stitch 6 bias squares to make a row, taking care to arrange them as shown. Press seams in one direction. Make 9 rows.

3. Stitch a row from step 2 between a 6½" x 10½" medium blue–print strip and a 1½" x 6½" medium blue–print strip. Press seams away from the bias square row. Make 9.

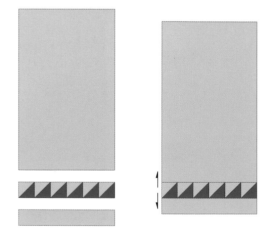

Assembling the Quilt

1. Arrange alternating half blocks and Sailboat blocks in 3 horizontal rows of 6 blocks each. Odd-numbered rows begin with half blocks, while even-numbered rows begin with Sailboat blocks.

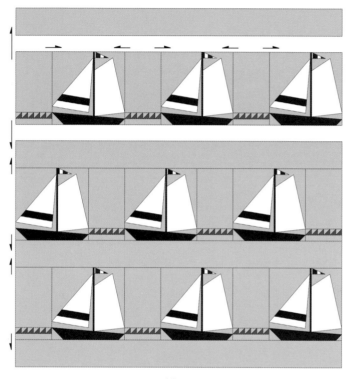

Assembly Diagram

2. Pin and sew the blocks together into rows. Press the seams toward the Sailboat blocks.

3. Refer to the assembly diagram and arrange alternating 5" x 54½", medium blue–print sashing strips and rows from step 2 as shown. Pin carefully. Sew the sashing strips and rows together. Press seams toward the sashing strips.

Adding the Borders

1. Divide two 2" x 44" inner border strips in half, and sew one half to each remaining 2" x 44" inner border strip.

2. Measure the quilt through its vertical center and trim 2 inner border strips to that measurement. Sew a trimmed border strip to opposite sides of the quilt. Press seams toward the border strips.

3. Measure the quilt through its horizontal center and trim the remaining 2 inner border strips to that measurement. Sew a trimmed border strip to the top and bottom of the quilt; press.

4. Sew a 3¼" x 57½" outer border strip to opposite sides of the quilt, and a 3¼" x 63" outer border strip to the top and bottom. Press seams toward the inner border.

FINISHING

1. Mark the quilt top with a design of your choice.

2. Layer the quilt top with batting and backing; baste.

3. Hand or machine quilt as desired.

4. Trim the backing and batting even with the edges of the quilt top. Cut 2¼"-wide bias strips from the 26" square of binding fabric for a total of approximately 260" of bias binding. Sew the binding to the quilt.

5. Make and attach a label to the quilt.

Seashore Dreamin'
Appliqué Patterns

Appliqué patterns do not include seam allowance.

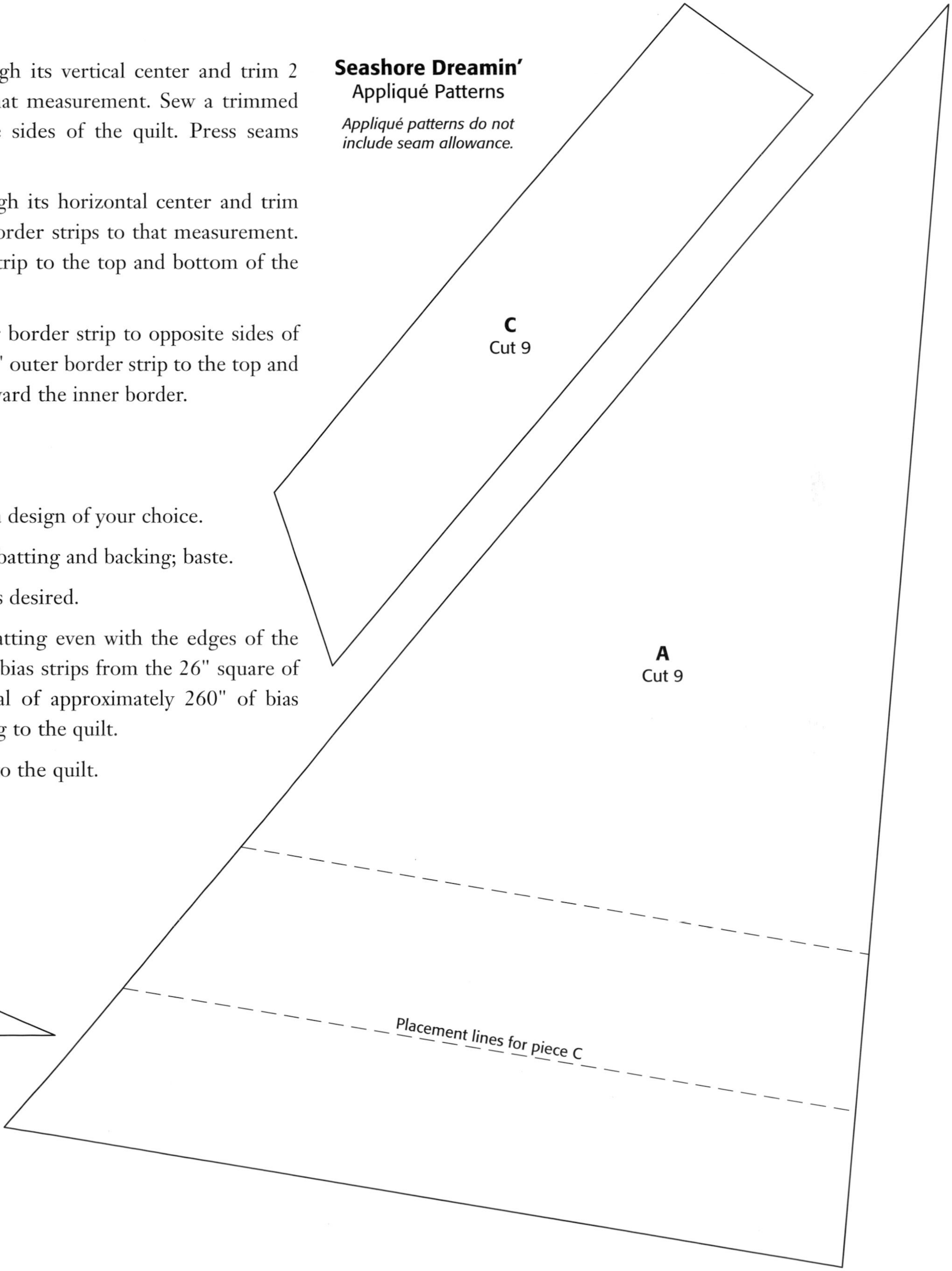

C
Cut 9

A
Cut 9

D
Cut 9

Placement lines for piece C

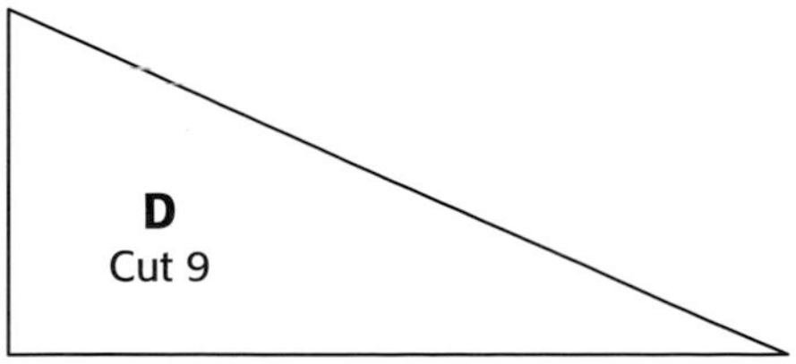

Seashore Dreamin'
Appliqué Pattern

Appliqué patterns do not include seam allowance.

B
Cut 9

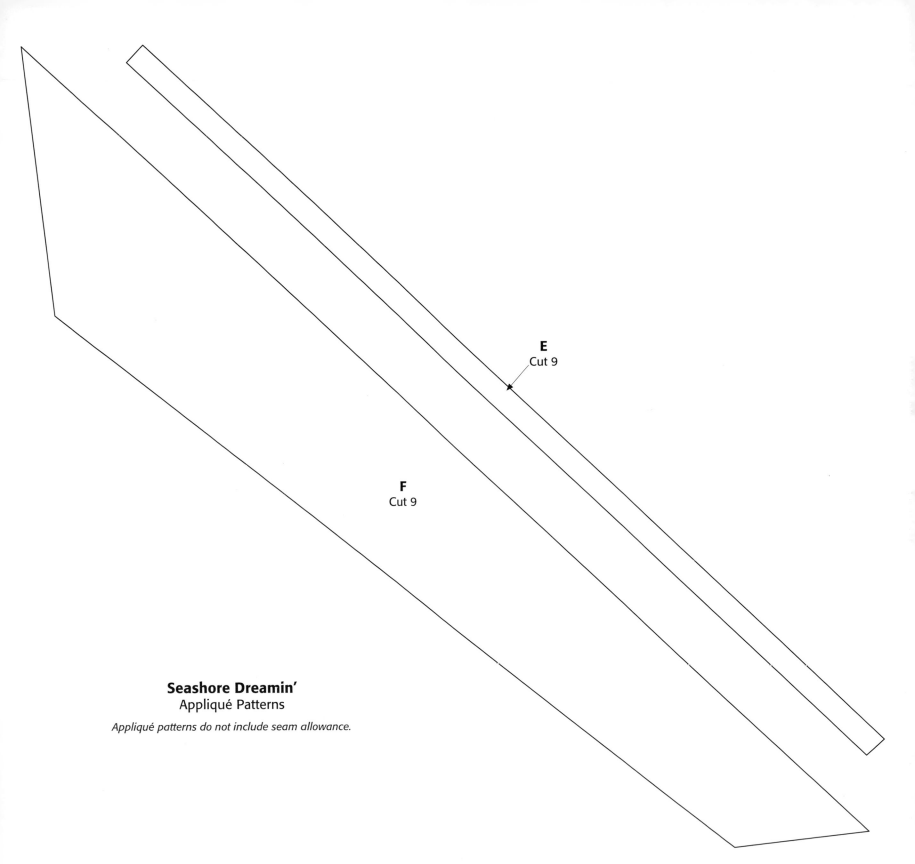

E
Cut 9

F
Cut 9

Seashore Dreamin'
Appliqué Patterns

Appliqué patterns do not include seam allowance.

*P*RETTY BASKETS OVERFLOWING *with late summer's harvest are a common sight at roadside stands and farmers' markets during the first crisp days of fall. Fresh flowers, herbs, and produce abound, while locally made wines and dairy products are favorite items for sampling.*

Baskets make wonderful serving pieces for picnics or other outdoor festivities. Whether you savor the season's bounty at a pregame tailgate party, a local soccer match, or a more elegant point de point, baskets can serve double duty, both for carrying food and serving it.

In Europe, school children are often seen in the market square, looking much like the charming French children depicted on the theme fabric used in our "Market Square" quilt. The fabric's warm hues balance nicely with the variety of cool, country blue prints used with it. You'll need only nine 16" blocks to make this adorable quilt—the perfect complement for an autumn picnic.

Picnic Potato Salad

INGREDIENTS

1 pound small new potatoes, unpeeled

½ cup mayonnaise

1 tablespoon white wine vinegar

1 ½ teaspoons Dijon mustard

1 tablespoon fresh tarragon

3 hard-boiled eggs, chopped

9-ounce jar marinated artichoke hearts, drained

1 tablespoon dill pickle, chopped

COOK potatoes until tender in a covered saucepan filled with water. Drain and cut into bite-size pieces. Combine mayonnaise, vinegar, mustard, and tarragon in a large bowl. Add eggs and artichokes. Fold in potatoes and pickle. Cover and chill for 24 hours.

YIELD: 4 SERVINGS.

MARKET SQUARE
by Nancy J. Martin, Woodinville, Washington, 2000. Quilted by Treva Mast, Millersburg, Ohio.

FINISHED QUILT SIZE: 60" x 60"
FINISHED BLOCK SIZE: 16" SQUARE

MATERIALS

44"-wide fabric

- 7 fat quarters of assorted light prints for blocks and pieced border
- 7 fat quarters of assorted blue prints for blocks and pieced border
- ⅜ yd. tan print for corner triangles
- ⅜ yd. medium blue subtle print for corner triangles
- ⅞ yd. theme print for block centers*
- ½ yd. light print for inner border
- 3¾ yds. fabric for backing
- 26" x 26" square of fabric for bias binding
- 64" x 64" square of lightweight batting

This yardage is based upon theme fabric cut on the straight grain, with no allowance for "fussy cutting." You may require additional fabric based on the size and number of repeats in your chosen theme fabric, and whether you plan to fussy-cut the theme motif.

CUTTING

All measurements include ¼"-side seam allowances. Use the pattern on page 77 to make the template for piece A.

From the assorted fat quarters of light prints, cut:
- A *total* of 18 squares, each 8" x 8", for bias squares
- A *total* of 54 squares, each 2⅞" x 2⅞". Cut each square once diagonally to make 108 triangles for blocks.
- A *total* of 25 squares, each 5¼" x 5¼". Cut each square twice diagonally to make 100 triangles for pieced borders.
- A *total* of 8 of piece A

From the assorted fat quarters of blue prints, cut:
- A *total* of 18 squares, each 8" x 8", for bias squares
- A *total* of 54 squares, each 2⅞" x 2⅞". Cut each square once diagonally to make 108 triangles for blocks.

- A *total* of 26 squares, each 5¼" x 5¼". Cut each square twice diagonally to make 108 triangles for pieced borders.

From the tan print, cut:
- 9 squares, each 6⅞" x 6⅞". Cut each square once diagonally to make 18 corner triangles.

From the medium blue subtle print, cut:
- 9 squares, each 6⅞" x 6⅞". Cut each square once diagonally to make 18 corner triangles.

From the theme print, cut:
- 9 squares, each 9" x 9", for block centers*

From the light print for inner border, cut:
- 6 strips, each 2½" x 44"

You may wish to center the theme print in the middle of each square.

NOTE: *Refer to "Quiltmaking Basics" on pages 119–127 for guidance as needed with all basic quiltmaking techniques.*

MAKING THE BLOCKS

YOU'LL NEED 9 blocks for this quilt.

1. Pair each 8" light square with an 8" blue square, right sides up. Cut and piece 2½"-wide bias strips (see page 119). Cut a total of 144 bias squares, each 2½" x 2½".

Cut 144 bias squares.

2. Arrange 2 bias squares, 1 small light-print triangle for blocks, and 3 small blue-print triangles as shown. Sew the bias squares and triangles together in rows. Press seams in opposite directions from row to row. Sew the rows together and press. Make 36.

Make 36.

3. Sew a unit from step 2 to each side of a 9" theme-print square. Press seams toward the theme square.

4. Arrange 2 bias squares and 2 small light-print triangles for blocks in a row. Sew the bias squares and triangles together; press. Make 36.

Make 36.

5. Sew a unit from step 4 to each side of a unit from step 3. Press seams away from the theme square.

6. Sew a medium blue, subtle-print triangle to the upper right and lower left corner of each unit from step 5. Press seams toward the blue triangles. Sew a tan-print triangle to the remaining sides of each unit; press.

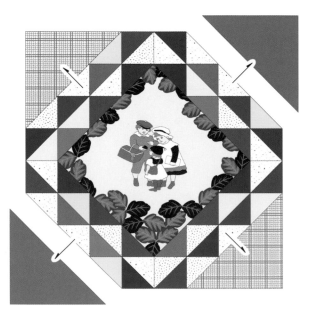

Assembling the Quilt

1. Arrange the blocks in 3 horizontal rows of 3 blocks each. Be sure to position blocks so that any fussy-cut center squares are oriented properly.

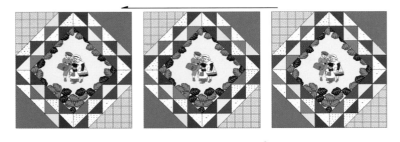
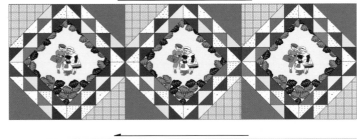

Assembly Diagram

2. Pin and then sew the blocks into rows. Press seams in opposite directions from row to row. Sew the rows together; press.

3. Divide two 2½" x 44" inner border strips in half, and sew one half to each remaining 2½" x 44" inner border strip.

4. Measure the quilt through its vertical center and trim 2 inner border strips to that measurement. Sew a trimmed border strip to opposite sides of the quilt. Press seams toward the border strips.

5. Measure the quilt through its horizontal center and trim the remaining 2 inner border strips to that measurement. Sew a trimmed border to the top and bottom of the quilt; press.

Making and Adding the Pieced Borders

1. Arrange and sew 14 assorted blue-print triangles and 13 assorted light-print triangles to make a pieced inner border row as shown. Press seams toward the darker triangles whenever possible. Make 4.

Make 4.

2. Arrange and sew 13 assorted blue-print triangles and 12 assorted light-print triangles to make a pieced outer border row as shown. Begin and end each row with a light-print piece A. Press seams toward the darker triangles whenever possible. Make 4.

Make 4.

3. With midpoints matching, sew a pieced inner border row from step 1 and a pieced outer border row from step 2 to make a pieced border unit as shown; press. Make 4.

Make 4.

4. Refer to the color photo on page 72. Taking care to position borders properly, sew a border unit to each side of the quilt. Miter the corners (see page 122), and press seams toward the light-print inner borders.

FINISHING

1. Mark the quilt top with a design of your choice.

2. Layer the quilt top with batting and backing; baste.

3. Hand or machine quilt as desired.

4. Trim the backing and batting even with the edges of the quilt top. Cut 2¼"-wide bias strips from the 26" square of binding fabric, for a total of approximately 250" of bias binding. Sew the binding to the quilt.

5. Make and attach a label to your quilt.

Butternut Bisque

INGREDIENTS

1 medium butternut squash (1 to 1 ½ pounds)

1 medium potato

1 ½ cups small French carrots

4 cups chicken stock

4 tablespoons (½ stick) butter

¼ cup flour

1/2 teaspoon salt

1 ½ teaspoons curry powder

¼ teaspoon nutmeg

½ cup heavy cream

PEEL and cube squash and potato; remove squash seeds. Place squash, potatoes, carrots, and stock in large stockpot. Cook over medium heat until the vegetables are tender (approximately 20 to 25 minutes). Remove vegetables, reserving liquid, and process in a food processor until smooth. Stir stock into puree and set aside. Use the same stockpot to melt butter. Add flour, salt, curry, and nutmeg, and stir until smooth. Add vegetable puree/stock mixture and heat until slightly thickened. Remove from heat, stir in cream, and serve. Transport this tasty bisque in a large thermos.

YIELD: 6 SERVINGS.

UNTIL THE PAPER GROCERY BAG WAS INTRODUCED SOMETIME AFTER 1865, STURDY BASKETS WERE A HOUSEHOLD NECESSITY. A VARIETY OF SPECIAL BASKETS WERE DESIGNED TO KEEP ITEMS SAFE EN ROUTE TO AND FROM THE MARKETPLACE. THERE WERE WOODEN BASKETS WITH WIRE FILIGREE SIDES FOR EGGS, TWIG BASKETS TO HOLD SMALL FOWL, AND LONG NARROW BASKETS USED BY THE FRENCH TO CARRY BAGUETTES.

IN THE LATE 1800S, THE FRENCH VILLAGE OF VALLABREGUES WAS HOME TO 450 BASKET MAKERS, AND WAS CONSIDERED THE CAPITAL OF FRENCH BASKETMAKING. ITS LOCATION ON A BEND OF THE RHÔNE RIVER PROVIDED AN ABUNDANCE OF RUSHES, REEDS, AND WILLOWS, MAKING IT AN IDEAL SPOT FOR THE "BANASTOUNIE," OR BASKET MAKER, TO PRACTICE HIS ART.

THE YOUNG, FLEXIBLE BRANCH OF THE WILLOW TREE WAS USED FOR WICKERWORK. BASKETS WOVEN FROM UNSTRIPPED BRANCHES (BARK STILL INTACT) RESULTED IN WICKERWORK WITH A RUSTIC APPEARANCE. FINE BASKETS WERE MADE OF BLOND WICKER, WHICH WAS STRIPPED OF ITS BARK AND RESULTED IN A VERY PALE BASKET THAT AGES TO A SOFT, STRAW-COLORED PATINA.

REEDS WERE USED TO WEAVE LARGE HAMPERS OR PANNIERS CALLED "BANASTES," AND LARGE CONICAL-SHAPED BASKETS WERE USED BY FISHERMEN TO TRAP FISH. ❧

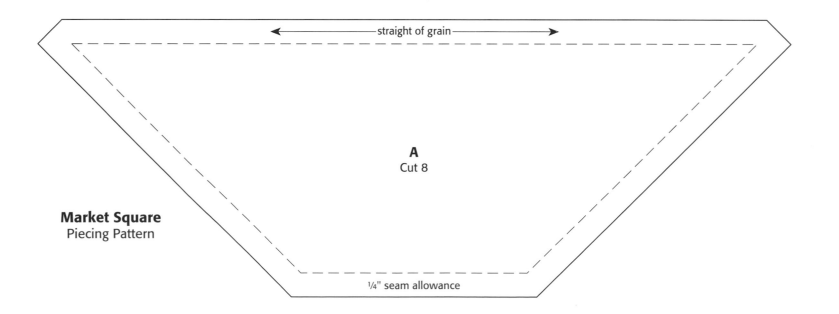

straight of grain

A
Cut 8

Market Square
Piecing Pattern

¼" seam allowance

Companion Project: Lined Picnic Basket

MATERIALS

44"-wide fabric

- Basket to be lined
- Piece of cardboard*
- Fabric #1 for liner*
- Fabric #2 (coordinating fabric) for liner trim*
- Piece of lightweight batting*
- Assorted buttons, trims, and ribbons (optional)
- Hot-glue gun

Yardages and/or size of these materials to be determined by the size of your basket.

CONSTRUCTING THE LINER

1. Cut 2 pieces of cardboard to the size and shape of the inside of the basket bottom. Use the cardboard to trace and cut 1 piece of batting to the same size and shape.

2. Trace the cardboard and cut 2 pieces of fabric #1 to the same size and shape plus 1" seam allowance for gluing.

3. Center 1 piece of cardboard wrong side up on the wrong side of one fabric #1 piece. Fold the excess fabric over the cardboard and hot glue in place.

4. Repeat step 3, sandwiching the batting between the remaining piece of cardboard and fabric. Hot glue in place.

LINED PICNIC BASKETS
by Suzette Halferty, Carnation, Washington, and Becky Hansen, Mukilteo, Washington, 2000.

5. Measure the circumference of the picnic basket and add seam allowances. Measure the depth of the basket and add at least 5". This additional fabric will help make the gluing process easier (see step 8) and allow you to fold the top edge of the lining over the edge of your basket. Cut a piece of fabric #1 to these measurements.

6. Cut a 4½"-wide strip of fabric #2. The *length* of this strip should equal the circumference of the basket plus ½". Sew the long side of this strip right sides together to the long side of the lining piece you cut in step 5; press.

7. Fold pieced lining unit from step 6 in half crosswise, right sides together, and stitch along short raw edges. Press; then turn the contrasting trim to the wrong side of the lining. Glue the raw edge of the trim to the wrong side of the lining.

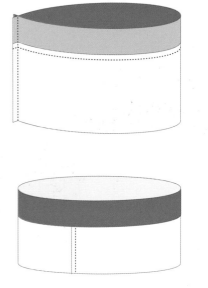

8. Turn cardboard unit from step 3 cardboard-side up. With the lining unit from step 7 wrong side out, hot glue the lining to the cardboard. Place cardboard with batting (step 4) fabric-side up inside the lining, and hot glue unit into the bottom.

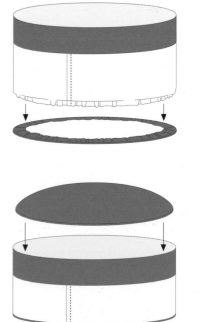

9. Place lining inside basket, folding the top edge over the basket edge. Fold the edge of the lining up so that the contrast fabric is visible. Decorate as desired with buttons, trims, and/or ribbons.

To CREATE AN alternate edging with triangles, measure the basket as in step 5 to determine the size of the lining piece, but add only 1" to the depth measurement of the basket— not 5"—for seam allowances and gluing. Cut 2 pairs of triangles from fabric that contrasts with the lining fabric. Cut the triangles so that 2 sides are shorter than the third side. Place the triangles right sides together, and stitch along the 2 short sides of the triangles. Turn the triangles right side out and press. In step 5, sew the triangles into the top-edge seam of the lining. To do this, pin the raw edge of the triangles to the long edge of the lining fabric. To determine triangle placement, find the center of your length of lining fabric. Center a triangle in each half of the lining, allowing ¼" for seam allowances at the outer edges of the lining. Place the 4½"-wide strip (see step 6) on top of the triangles, right sides facing, and sew layers together. Continue with steps 7–9.

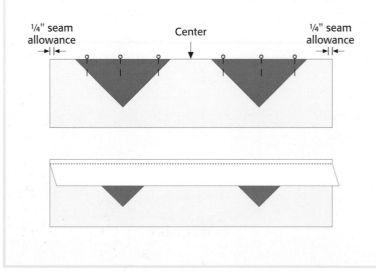

*A*s the rich *palette of autumn infuses the surrounding landscape, it is hard to imagine that the climax of color will soon be replaced by the winter's stark scenery. The countryside is plentiful with fields of golden pumpkins and squash, the orchards are full of juicy red and green apples, and tawny nuts fall from their trees. Once again, we are reminded of nature's bounty, and seek to enjoy the harvest with family and friends.*

Sweet Hazelnut Pound Cake is the perfect snack to accompany a drive in the country. Coupled with a thermos of hot coffee or tea, it makes the ideal refreshment for a brisk, bonfire-scented afternoon.

"Indian Summer," abundant with autumnal fabrics, will keep October memories alive through January snows. Based on the traditional Indian Mat and Indian Squares blocks, this easy-to-assembly quilt is sure to become a treasured heirloom.

Sweet Hazelnut Pound Cake

INGREDIENTS

1 ¾ cups all-purpose flour

½ teaspoon baking powder

½ teaspoon nutmeg

½ teaspoon cinnamon

¼ pound plus 4 tablespoons (1 ½ sticks) butter, softened

1 ½ cups sugar

3 eggs

1 teaspoon vanilla extract

½ cup buttermilk

1 pound cooked acorn squash, pureed and cooled

½ cup chopped hazelnuts

PREHEAT oven to 350°. Butter and flour a 12" bundt pan or a 9" x 5" x 3" loaf pan. In a small bowl, mix flour, baking powder, nutmeg, and cinnamon together; set aside. Cream sugar and butter together in a mixing bowl; then add eggs one at a time, blending well after each. Stir in vanilla. Slowly add buttermilk, alternating with the dry ingredients. Fold in the squash and hazelnuts last. Pour batter into prepared pan and bake for 50 to 60 minutes, or until toothpick inserted in the center comes out clean.

YIELD: 18 SERVINGS.

Indian Summer

INDIAN SUMMER
by Suzette Halferty, Carnation, Washington, 1999. Quilted by Emma Shetler, Charm, Ohio.

FINISHED QUILT SIZE: 76" x 76"

FINISHED BLOCK SIZE: 12" SQUARE

MATERIALS

44"-wide fabric

- 2 yds. beige print for blocks, nine-patch unit, and pieced setting triangles
- ½ yd. dark print for blocks
- ¼ yd. rust print #1 for blocks
- ⅜ yd. rust print #2 for blocks
- ½ yd. dark brown print for blocks
- 4 yds. rust print #3 for blocks, nine-patch unit, pieced setting triangles, and border
- 4½ yds. fabric for backing
- 30" x 30" square of fabric for bias binding
- 80" x 80" square of lightweight batting

CUTTING

All measurements include ¼"-wide seam allowances.

From the beige print, cut:
- 1 fat quarter, 18" x 22", for bias squares
- 4 squares, each 2⅞" x 2⅞". Cut each square once diagonally to make 8 small triangles for blocks.
- 16 strips, each 6½" x 12½", for blocks
- 4 squares, each 13¼" x 13¼". Cut each square twice diagonally to make 16 large triangles for blocks and pieced setting triangles.
- 4 squares, each 9" x 9", for nine-patch unit
- 2 squares, each 6⅞" x 6⅞". Cut each square once diagonally to make 4 corner triangles.

From the dark print, cut:
- 1 fat quarter, 18" x 22", for bias squares
- 4 squares, each 2⅞" x 2⅞". Cut each square once diagonally to make 8 triangles for blocks.

From rust print #1, cut:
- 4 squares, each 6½" x 6½", for blocks

From rust print #2, cut:
- 8 squares, each 5⅛" x 5⅛". Cut each square once diagonally to make 16 triangles for blocks.

From the dark brown print, cut:
- 8 squares, each 6⅞" x 6⅞". Cut each square once diagonally to make 16 triangles for blocks.

From rust print #3, cut:
- 9 squares, each 9" x 9", for nine-patch unit and pieced setting triangles
- 2 border strips, each 8¼" x 60½", along the *lengthwise* grain
- 2 border strips, each 8¼" x 76", along the *lengthwise* grain

NOTE: *Refer to "Quiltmaking Basics" on pages 119–127 for guidance as needed with all basic quiltmaking techniques.*

MAKING THE BLOCKS

YOU'LL NEED 4 Indian Mat blocks for this quilt.

1. Pair the beige-print fat quarter with the dark-print fat quarter, right sides up. Cut and piece 2½"-wide bias strips (see page 119). *Press seams open.* Cut 48 bias squares, each 2½" x 2½".

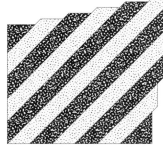 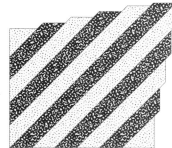

2. Sew 3 bias square units to make a row, positioning them as shown. Press seams to one side. Make 8.

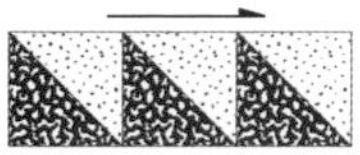

Make 8.

3. Sew a dark-print triangle, 3 bias squares, and a small beige-print triangle to make a row, positioning them as shown; press. Make 8.

Make 8.

4. Sew a row from step 2 to opposite sides of each 6½" rust print #1 square, positioning the bias squares as shown. Press seams toward the pieced rows. Make 4.

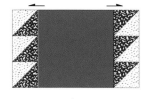

Make 4.

5. Sew a row from step 3 to the remaining sides of each unit from step 4 as shown. Press seams toward the center square.

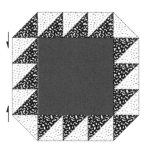

6. Sew a rust print #2 triangle to each side of the block. Press seams toward the corner triangles.

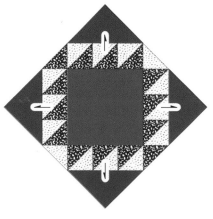

Block Assembly Diagram

Assembling the Quilt

1. Arrange and sew an Indian Mat block, two 6½" x 12½" beige-print strips, and a large beige print triangle to make a vertical row as shown. Press seams away from the block. Make 4.

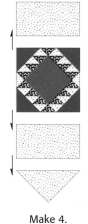

Make 4.

2. Sew a remaining 6½" x 12½" beige-print strip between 2 dark brown triangles as shown. Press seams toward the triangles. Make 8.

Make 8.

3. Sew a remaining large beige-print triangle to a unit from step 2 as shown. Press seams toward the beige triangle. Make 4.

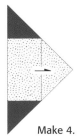

Make 4.

4. Sew a unit from step 1 between a unit from step 2 and step 3 as shown. Press seams away from the center unit. Make 4.

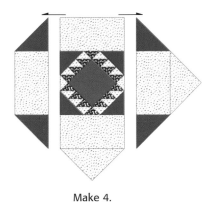

Make 4.

5. Arrange five 9" rust-print #3 squares and four 9" beige-print squares to make a nine-patch unit as shown. Sew the squares into rows, and press seams in opposite directions from row to row. Sew the rows together; press. Make 1.

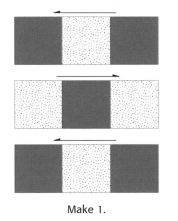

Make 1.

6. Arrange a remaining 9" rust-print #3 square and 2 large beige-print triangles as shown. Sew the triangles to adjacent sides of the square. Press seams away from the square. Make 4 pieced setting triangles.

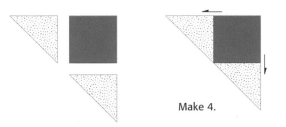

Make 4.

7. Arrange the "framed" Indian Mat blocks, nine-patch unit, pieced setting triangles, and small beige-print corner triangles as shown below.

8. Pin; then sew the blocks, nine-patch unit, pieced setting triangles, and corner triangles to make 3 diagonal rows as shown. Press seams in opposite directions from row to row. Sew the rows together; press.

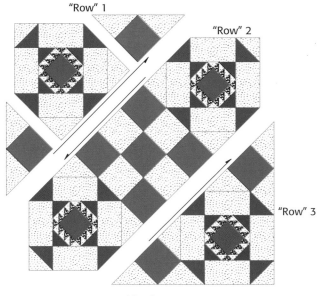

Assembly Diagram

9. Sew an 8¼" x 60½" border strip to opposite sides of the quilt. Press seams toward the border strips. Sew an 8¼" x 76" strip to the top and bottom of the quilt; press.

FINISHING

1. Mark the quilt top with a design of your choice.

2. Layer the quilt top with batting and backing; baste.

3. Hand or machine quilt as desired.

4. Trim the backing and batting even with the edges of the quilt top. Cut 2¼"-wide bias strips from the 30" square of binding fabric, for a total of approximately 314" of bias binding. Sew the binding to the quilt.

5. Make and attach a label to your quilt.

T HE WINTER HOLIDAYS *inspire wonderful gatherings, and the season would be incomplete without an outing to search for the perfect Christmas tree. Family and friends, bundled in heavy coats, mittens, and boots, gather to warm themselves with hot-spiced cider, to swap holiday stories, and to reminisce over favorite childhood memories. "Christmas Tree Farm" reminds us that such events are at the heart of the holiday season. Imagine the warmth and joy this quilt will bring as it extends the magic of the holidays all winter long.*

Tree Hunter's Stew

INGREDIENTS

¼ cup flour

1 teaspoon chili powder

1 teaspoon ground cinnamon

1 tablespoon brown sugar

1½ teaspoons salt

½ teaspoon freshly ground black pepper

3 pounds lean beef stew meat, cut into 1" cubes

¼ cup olive oil

3 small shallots, finely sliced

¼ cup brandy

⅓ cup balsamic vinegar

1 cup beef stock

2½ cups sliced mushrooms

COMBINE flour, chili powder, cinnamon, brown sugar, salt, and pepper in a plastic resealable bag. Add beef and shake to coat. Heat 2 tablespoons of the ¼ cup of olive oil in a skillet over medium high heat. Brown beef in batches, adding oil as needed, and transferring each browned batch to a dutch oven or casserole dish. Reduce heat to medium, and add final tablespoon of olive oil. Add shallots and cook until lightly browned. Add brandy and reduce by half. Stir shallots into meat; then add vinegar, beef stock, and mushrooms. Bake at 350°, covered, about 2½ hours, or until beef is tender. Uncover and bake for another 30 minutes.

YIELD: 6 SERVINGS.

CHRISTMAS TREE FARM

by Nancy J. Martin, Woodinville, Washington, 1999. Quilted by Miriam Yoder, Charm, Ohio.

FINISHED QUILT SIZE: 59¾" x 59¾"
FINISHED BLOCK SIZE: 10" SQUARE

MATERIALS

44"-wide fabric

- 2⅜ yds. *total* light flannel prints for pieced and appliquéd blocks, setting and corner triangles, and inner border
- ¾ yd. *each* of 4 green flannel prints for trees and leaves*
- ⅜ yd. medium brown flannel print for moose appliqués and tree trunks
- 1 fat quarter light brown flannel print for moose appliqués
- 1 fat quarter cranberry flannel print for bird appliqués
- ¼ yd. green flannel print for vines
- 1¼ yds. plaid flannel for outer border and yo-yo berries
- 26" x 26" square of fabric for bias binding
- 3¾ yds. fabric for backing
- 64" x 64" piece of batting

Yardage measurements are based on making 2 trees from each green print, plus 1 extra tree from your favorite green print.

CUTTING

All measurements include ¼"-wide seam allowances. Use the pattern on page 95 to make a template for piece D.

From the light flannel prints, cut:
- A *total* of 45 squares, each 2⅞" x 2⅞". Cut each square once diagonally to make 90 triangles for tree blocks.
- A *total* of 9 squares, each 8" x 8", for bias squares
- A *total* of 9 squares, each 2⅜" x 2⅜". Cut each square once diagonally to make 18 triangles for tree blocks.
- A *total* of 18 strips, each 2" x 6½", for tree blocks
- A *total* of 4 squares, each 11" x 11", for appliqué blocks
- A *total* of 2 squares, each 15½" x 15½". Cut each square twice diagonally to make 8 side setting triangles.
- A *total* of 2 squares, each 8" x 8". Cut each square once diagonally to make 4 corner triangles.

- A *total* of 5 matching strips, each 4" x 44", for inner border

From *each* of the 4 green flannel prints, cut:
- 2 squares (8 total), each 5¼"x 5¼". Cut each square twice diagonally to make 32 large triangles for tree blocks.
- 2 squares (8 total), each 8" x 8", for bias squares
- 4 squares (16 total), each 2⅞" x 2⅞". Cut each square once diagonally to make 32 small triangles for tree blocks.

From your favorite green flannel print, cut:
- 1 square, 5¼" x 5¼". Cut twice diagonally to make 4 large triangles for tree blocks.
- 1 square, 8" x 8", for bias squares
- 2 squares, each 2⅞" x 2⅞". Cut each square once diagonally to make 4 small triangles for tree blocks.

From the medium brown flannel print, cut:
- 9 strips, each 1½" x 6½", for tree blocks

From the green flannel print for vines, cut:
- 14 bias strips, each 1¼" x 10½"

From the plaid flannel fabric, cut:
- 16 of piece D
- 6 strips, each 5¼" x 44", for outer border

NOTE: *Refer to "Quiltmaking Basics" on pages 119–127 for guidance as needed with all basic quiltmaking techniques.*

Making the Tree Blocks

You'll need 9 Tree blocks for this quilt. Each tree is made from a single green print.

1. Sew a 2⅞" light-print triangle to each short side of a large green-print triangle to make a Flying Geese unit. Press seams toward light triangles. Make 27.

Make 27.

2. Arrange 3 Flying Geese units and a large green-print triangle in a vertical row as shown. Sew the units and triangle together, and press seams in one direction. Make 9.

Make 9.

3. Pair each 8" light-print square with an 8" green-print square, right sides up. Cut and piece 2½"-wide bias strips (see page 119). Cut 72 bias squares, each 2½" x 2½".

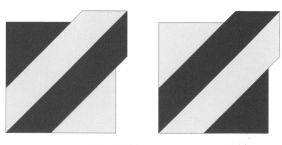

Cut 72 bias squares.

4. Arrange 3 bias squares, 2 small green-print triangles, and a 2⅜" light-print triangle, positioning them as shown. Sew the bias squares and triangles into rows; press seams in opposite directions from row to row. Sew the rows together; press. Make 9. Repeat to make 9 reversed units as shown; press.

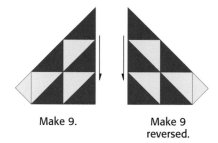

Make 9.   Make 9
                 reversed.

5. Sew a unit from step 2 between a regular and reverse unit from step 4 as shown. Press seams away from the center unit. Make 9.

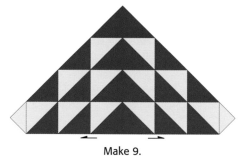

Make 9.

6. Arrange four 2⅞" light-print triangles, 2 bias squares, two 2" x 6½" light-print strips, and a 1½" x 6½" medium brown-print strip as shown. Sew the units and pieces together. Press seams toward the brown strip. Make 9.

Make 9.

7. Sew units from step 5 and step 6 together in pairs as shown in the block assembly diagram below. Press seams toward the bottom unit.

8. Use a quilter's ruler to square the bottom corner of the block, leaving a ¼" seam allowance.

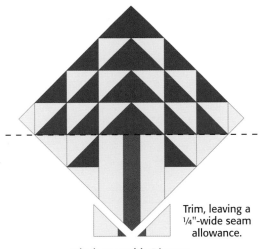

Trim, leaving a ¼"-wide seam allowance.

Block Assembly Diagram

APPLIQUÉING THE BLOCKS

1. Use the patterns on pages 94–95 to make templates for appliqué pieces A–C. Trace the templates to cut 1 each of piece A regular and A reversed from both the light brown and medium brown prints (4 total), a total of 60 of piece B from the assorted green prints, and 1 each of piece C regular and C reversed from the cranberry print. Set all but pieces A regular and A reversed aside for now.

2. Fold each 11" light-print square twice diagonally to find its center point; crease lightly and unfold. Refer to the color photo on page 88. Turn each square on point, and stitch one piece A regular or A reversed appliqué in place. Trim blocks to 10½" x 10½" when appliqué is completed.

ASSEMBLING THE QUILT

1. Arrange the pieced and appliquéd blocks, and the light-print side setting and corner triangles in diagonal rows as shown.

2. Pin and then sew the blocks and triangles together to make 7 diagonal rows. Press seams in opposite directions from row to row. Sew the rows together; press.

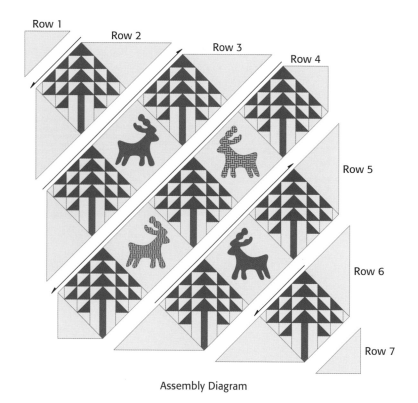

Assembly Diagram

3. Measure the quilt through its vertical center and trim two 4" x 44" light-print inner border strips to that measurement. Sew a trimmed border strip to opposite sides of the quilt. Press seams toward the border strips.

4. Divide one 4" x 44" light-print inner border strip in half, and sew one half to each remaining 4" x 44" inner border strip.

5. Measure the quilt through its horizontal center and trim the 2 pieced inner border strips to that measurement. Sew a trimmed border strip to the top and bottom of the quilt; press.

6. Refer to "Bias-Strip Appliqué" on page 121. Seam the 1¼"-wide green bias strips together to make 2 vine segments, each approximately 72" long. Refer to the color photo on page 88 and appliqué a vine segment to the upper left and lower right corners of the quilt. Appliqué 30 leaves (piece B) to each vine.

7. Use each piece D to make a yo-yo berry. Thread a needle with a double length of sewing thread; knot the ends. Turn raw edge to the wrong side of the fabric circle, making a ¼" hem, and take a running stitch through all thicknesses a scant ¼" from the edge, all around the circle. Gently pull the thread and gather the circle into a pouch, right side out. Use your fingers to flatten, smooth, and center the gathered fabric. Take a few stitches through the center and tie off on the gathered side. Make 16.

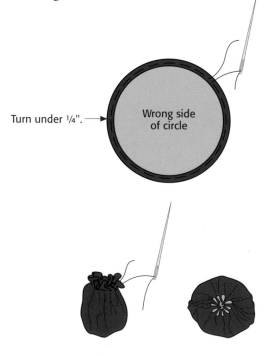

Turn under ¼".

Wrong side of circle

8. Refer to the color photo on page 88 and appliqué 8 yo-yo berries to each vine. Stitch a bird (piece C regular or C reversed) to each appliquéd corner.

9. Sew 5¼" x 44" plaid outer border strips end to end to make a continuous 5¼"-wide outer border strip. Measure the quilt through its vertical center and cut 2 outer border strips to that measurement. Sew a trimmed border strip to opposite sides of the quilt. Press seams toward the border strips.

10. Measure the quilt through its horizontal center and cut 2 outer border strips to that measurement. Sew a trimmed border strip to the top and bottom of the quilt; press.

FINISHING

1. Mark the quilt top with a design of your choice.

2. Layer the quilt top with batting and backing; baste.

3. Hand or machine quilt as desired.

4. Trim the backing and batting even with the edges of the quilt top. Cut 2¼"-wide bias strips from the 26" square of binding fabric, for a total of approximately 275" of bias binding. Sew the binding to the quilt.

5. Make and attach a label to your quilt.

Mulled Wine

INGREDIENTS

2 cinnamon sticks
10 whole cloves
10 allspice berries
1 dried orange peel
½ gallon of red wine

COMBINE all ingredients in a large pot or kettle. Heat slowly, and allow to steep for ½ hour. Serve warm in mugs with handles.

YIELD: ½ GALLON; 6 TO 8 SERVINGS.

Spiced Cider

INGREDIENTS

1 gallon apple juice or apple cider
2 cinnamon sticks, crushed
10 whole cloves
10 allspice berries
1 dried orange peel
½ teaspoon nutmeg
Whole cinnamon sticks for garnish

COMBINE all ingredients in a large pot or kettle. Stir; then heat slowly, allowing the flavors to blend for at least 1 hour before serving. Ladle into mugs with handles, and garnish with a whole cinnamon stick.

YIELD: 1 GALLON; 12 TO 16 SERVINGS.

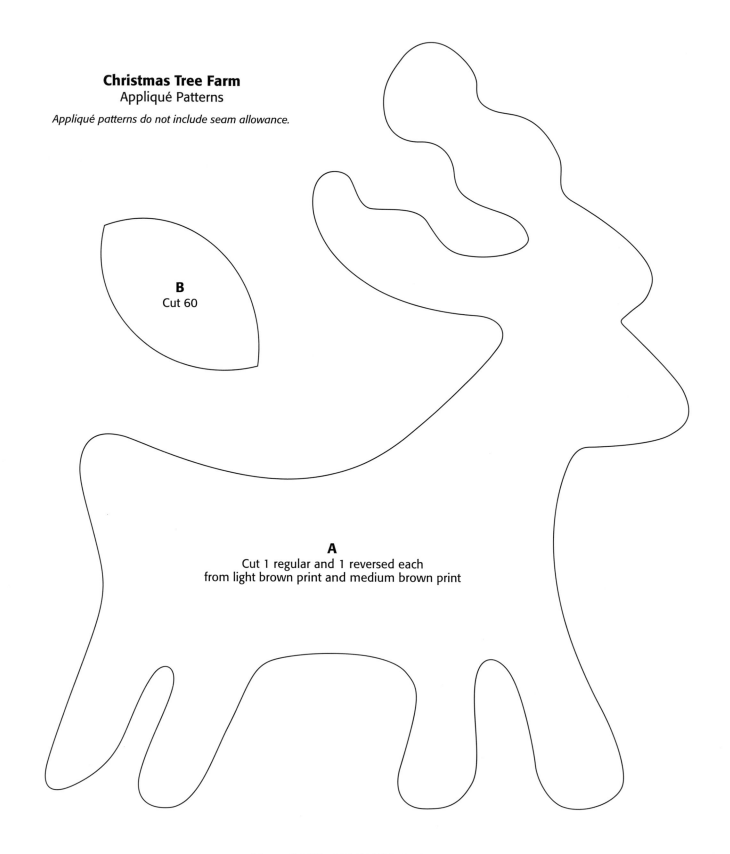

Christmas Tree Farm
Appliqué Patterns

Appliqué patterns do not include seam allowance.

B
Cut 60

A
Cut 1 regular and 1 reversed each
from light brown print and medium brown print

Christmas Tree Farm
Appliqué and Yo-yo Patterns

Appliqué patterns do not include seam allowance.

C
Cut 1 regular and 1 reversed

D
Cut 16

Includes seam allowance.

W HAT BETTER TIME *than New Year's Eve to retreat to the warmth of a cozy boudoir for a romantic indoor picnic? The simple joy of sharing quiet, candlelit time with someone special is perfect for unwinding after the hectic holiday season.*

Lovely to look at, "Champagne Elegance" evokes a formal sophistication that even the beginning quilter will welcome. Alternating blocks in a champagne and cocoa-colored scheme are linked with small appliqués; then the quilt is gracefully quilted with a classy, curving motif. Whether tossed over a sofa, gracing a bed, or adorning a wall, "Champagne Elegance" adds romance to any setting.

Potted Beef Pâté

INGREDIENTS

1 pound good stewing beef, cut in 1" cubes
½ teaspoon freshly ground black pepper
¼ teaspoon salt
¼ teaspoon nutmeg
½ teaspoon tarragon
1 tablespoon anchovy paste
¼ pound (1 stick) unsalted butter, melted
12 toasted baguette slices

PLACE beef in an ovenproof pan with a tight-fitting lid. Stir pepper, salt, nutmeg, tarragon, and anchovy paste into melted butter and pour over meat. Cover and cook in a 275° oven for 5 hours, stirring after 2 hours. Let cool slightly; then process in a food processor until smooth. Spread on baguette slices and serve, if desired, with a glass of champagne.

YIELD: 6 SERVINGS.

THIS pâté keeps well for a few days when stored in a glass jar in the refrigerator. If you wish to keep it longer (up to a week) or take it on a picnic, seal the jar with clarified butter.

Champagne Elegance

CHAMPAGNE ELEGANCE
by Suzette Halferty, Carnation, Washington, 2000.

FINISHED SIZE: 60" x 60"

MATERIALS

44"-wide fabric

- 2¾ yds. cream print for blocks, setting triangles, and inner and outer borders
- 1 yd. cocoa print for blocks and setting triangles
- ⅝ yd. black print for middle border, and A and B appliqués
- 3¾ yds. fabric for backing
- 26" x 26" square of cocoa print for bias binding*
- 64" x 64" piece of lightweight batting

*Can be same print used for blocks.

CUTTING

All measurements include ¼"-wide seam allowances.

From the cream print, cut:
- 12 squares, each 7½" x 7½", for blocks
- 2 squares, each 11¼" x 11¼". Cut each square twice diagonally to make 8 setting triangles.
- 6 strips, each 1¼ x 44", for inner border
- 6 strips, each 8¼" x 44", for outer border

From the cocoa print for blocks and setting triangles, cut:
- 12 squares, each 7½" x 7½", for blocks
- 2 squares, each 11¼" x 11¼". Cut each square twice diagonally to make 8 setting triangles.

From the black print, cut:
- 16 squares, each 2" x 2", for piece A
- 6 strips, each 2" x 44", for middle border

NOTE: *Refer to "Quiltmaking Basics" on pages 119–127 for guidance as needed with all basic quiltmaking techniques.*

ASSEMBLING THE QUILT

1. Arrange the 7½" cream-print and cocoa-print blocks and the cream-print and cocoa-print setting triangles, in diagonal rows as shown.

2. Pin and then sew the blocks and triangles together to make 8 diagonal rows. Press seams in opposite directions from row to row. Sew the rows together; press.

3. Divide two 1¼" x 44" cream-print inner border strips in half, and sew one half to each remaining 1¼" x 44" inner border strip. Repeat for the 2" x 44" black-print middle border strips and the 8¼" x 44" cream-print outer border strips.

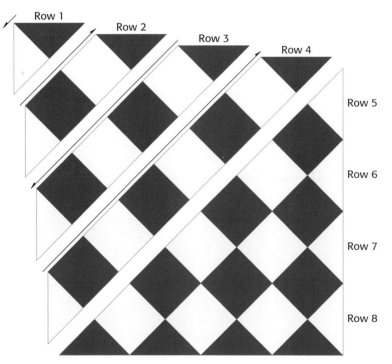

Assembly Diagram

4. Refer to the color photo on page 98, and sew a pieced 1¼"-wide inner border strip, 2"-wide middle border strip, and 8¼"-wide outer border strip as shown. Press seams toward the middle border strip. Make 4 border units.

5. Measure, trim, and sew a border unit to each side of the quilt. Miter the corners (see page 122).

ADDING THE APPLIQUÉS

1. Use the pattern on page 102 to make a template for piece B. Trace the template to cut 4 of piece B from the remaining black print.

2. Refer to the color photo on page 98, and appliqué a piece A (square) at the intersection of each cream and cocoa square. Appliqué a piece B (diamond) at the center of each outer border strip.

FINISHING

1. Mark the quilt top with a design of your choice. If you wish, you may use the quilting motifs on pages 102–103. The quilting diagram on page 101 indicates how to place them.

2. Layer the quilt top with batting and backing; baste.

3. Using thread of a contrasting color, hand or machine quilt as desired.

4. Trim the backing and batting even with the edges of the quilt top. Cut 2¼"-wide bias strips from the 26" square of cocoa-print binding fabric, for a total of approximately 250" of bias binding. Sew the binding to the quilt.

5. Make and attach a label to your quilt.

Quilting Diagram

A SPECIAL GATHERING *of friends adds much-needed warmth to a home under construction. Sawhorses provide the perfect base for a makeshift buffet table, canned and bottled beverages are easily chilled in ice-filled aluminum buckets, and the beat of "boom-box" jazz tempers the sound of hammers in the background.*

By featuring gentle floral fabrics rather than the expected calicoes, our casually elegant "Dream House" quilt transforms a well-loved classic pattern into something fresh and new. This unique coupling adds just the right mix of old-fashioned style and sophisticated charm to any new home.

Builder's Bruschetta

INGREDIENTS

One 14 oz. baguette, cut into ¾"-thick slices
(approximately 24 slices)
3 to 4 cloves garlic, smashed with side of knife
¼ cup olive oil
2 cups Roma tomatoes, seeded, finely chopped, and drained
½ cup shredded mozzarella cheese
⅓ cup fresh basil, chopped
2 cloves garlic, finely minced
2 tablespoons kalamata olives, finely minced
2 tablespoons red onion, finely minced
2 tablespoons balsamic vinegar
½ teaspoon salt

RUB one side of bread slices with smashed garlic; broil or grill both sides until brown. Lightly brush one side of toasted bread slices with olive oil; set aside remaining olive oil. In a bowl, mix tomatoes, mozarella cheese, basil, minced garlic, olives, and red onion. In a second bowl, whisk remaining olive oil, balsamic vinegar, and salt; pour over tomato mixture and mix. Spoon onto toasted bread just before serving.

YIELD: 12 SERVINGS.

Dream House

DREAM HOUSE
by Nancy J. Martin, Woodinville, Washington, 1999. Quilted by Elsie Mast, Charm, Ohio.

Finished Quilt Size: 60" x 60"
Finished Block Size: 12" square

Materials

44"-wide fabric

NOTE: *Five fat quarter packets were used in the construction of the quilt shown on page 106. Each contained 6 fat quarters of coordinating fabrics in a single pastel color (pink, yellow, blue, mint, and sage green). Two houses each of pink, yellow, mint, and blue surround a single sage green house. Corresponding prints were used consistently in each house. Cutting directions specify which part of the house was from each type of print. If you can't find 5 coordinating fat quarter packets, have fun making up your own!*

- 5 fat quarter packets, each containing 6 coordinating fabrics in a single color: pink, yellow, mint green, blue, and sage green (a total of 30 different fabrics)
- 1½ yds. large-scale coordinating print for border
- 26" x 26" square of fabric for bias binding
- 3¾ yd. fabric for backing
- 64" x 64" piece of lightweight batting

Cutting

All measurements include ¼"-wide seam allowances. Use patterns on pages 110–111 to make templates for pieces A–D.

From the 6 fat quarters of pink fabric, cut:
- Fabric #1 (small, light, allover print for background/sky)
    - 2 regular and 2 reversed of piece D
    - 2 of piece B
    - 2 strips, each 2½" x 4½"
    - 4 squares, each 2½" x 2½"
    - 4 strips, each 1½" x 6½"
    - 4 strips, each 1½" x 7½"
- Fabric #2 (subtle striped floral for left side of house)
    - 4 strips, each 1½" x 4½", with stripes running horizontally

- 4 strips, each 1½" x 4½", with stripes running vertically
    - 2 of piece C
- Fabric #3 (solid)
    - 2 strips, each 2½" x 4½", for doors
    - 4 strips, each 2½" x 3½", for windows
- Fabric #4 (medium-scale print for roof)
    - 2 of piece A
- Fabric #5 (small-scale floral print)
    - 6 strips, each 1½" x 3½", for right side of house
    - 4 strips, each 1½" x 7½", for right side of house
    - 4 squares, each 2½" x 2½", for chimneys
- Fabric #6 (tone-on-tone print)
    - 9 strips, each 2" x 12½", for sashing
    - 9 squares, each 2" x 2", for corner squares

Repeat for the packets of yellow, mint green, and blue fabrics.

From the 6 fat quarters of sage green fabrics, cut:
- Fabric #1 (small, light, allover print for background/sky)
    - 1 regular and 1 reversed of piece D
    - 1 of piece B
    - 1 strip, 2½" x 4½"
    - 2 squares, each 2½" x 2½"
    - 2 strips, each 1½" x 6½"
    - 2 strips, each 1½" x 7½"
- Fabric #2 (subtle striped floral for left side of house)
    - 2 strips, each 1½" x 4½", with stripes running horizontally
    - 2 strips, each 1½" x 4½", with stripes running vertically
    - 1 of piece C
- Fabric #3 (solid)
    - 1 strip, 2½" x 4½", for door
    - 2 strips, each 2½" x 3½", for windows
- Fabric #4 (medium-scale print for roof)
    - 1 piece A
- Fabric #5 (small-scale floral print)
    - 3 strips, each 1½" x 3½", for right side of house
    - 2 strips, each 1½" x 7½", for right side of house
    - 2 squares, each 2½" x 2½", for chimneys

From the coordinating large-scale print, cut:

6 strips, each 7¾" x 44", for border

NOTE: *Refer to "Quiltmaking Basics" on pages 119–127 for guidance as needed with all basic quiltmaking techniques.*

PIECING THE BLOCKS

YOU'LL NEED 9 House blocks for this quilt. You'll be constructing 2 houses each from the pink, yellow, blue, and mint green fabrics, and 1 from the sage green fabrics.

For each house:

1. Refer to the diagram below, and use 1 each of pieces A, B, C, D regular and D reversed, two 2½" fabric #5 squares, two 2½" fabric #1 squares, and one 2½" x 4½" fabric #1 strip as shown to construct the top half of each house block. Press as desired.

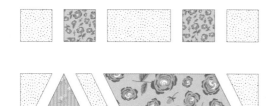

2. Refer to the diagram below, and use one 1½" x 6½" and one 1½" x 7½" fabric #1 strip; 2 horizontal and 2 vertical 1½" x 4½" fabric #2 strips; one 2½" x 4½" and two 2½" x 3½" fabric #3 strips; and three 1½" x 3½" and two 1½" x 7½" fabric #5 strips as shown to construct the bottom half of each house block. Press as desired.

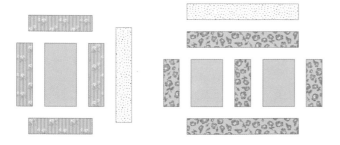

3. Sew a unit from step 1 to a unit with matching colors from step 2 as shown. Press seams toward the bottom unit.

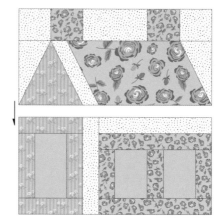

4. Frame each block with four 2" fabric #6 squares and four 2" x 12½" fabric #6 strips in the colors shown. Press seams toward the framing strips.

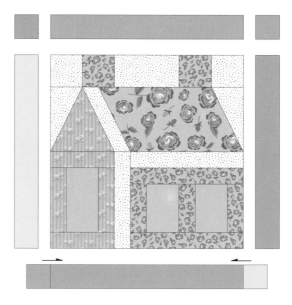

Assembling the Quilt

1. Arrange the framed blocks in 3 horizontal rows of 3 blocks each, placing the sage green block in the middle of the quilt as shown. Sew the blocks together into rows. Press seams in opposite directions from row to row.

2. Sew the rows together; press.

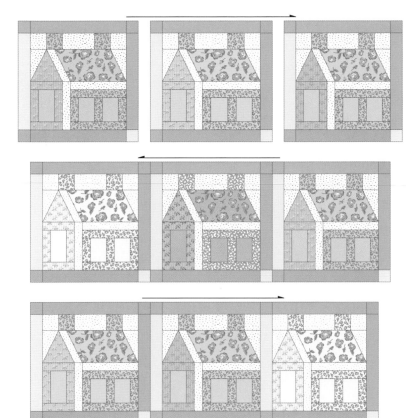

Assembly Diagram

3. Divide two 7¾" x 44" large-scale print border strips in half, and sew one half to each remaining 7¾" x 44" border strip.

4. Measure the quilt through its vertical center and trim 2 borders to that measurement. Sew a trimmed border strip to opposite sides of the quilt. Press seams toward the border strips.

5. Measure the quilt through its horizontal center and trim 2 border strips to that measurement. Sew a trimmed border to the top and bottom of the quilt; press.

Finishing

1. Mark the quilt top with a design of your choice.

2. Layer the quilt top with batting and backing; baste.

3. Hand or machine quilt as desired.

4. Trim the backing and batting even with the edges of the quilt top. Cut 2¼"-wide bias strips from the 26" square of binding fabric, for a total of approximately 250" of bias binding. Sew the binding to the quilt.

5. Make and attach a label to your quilt.

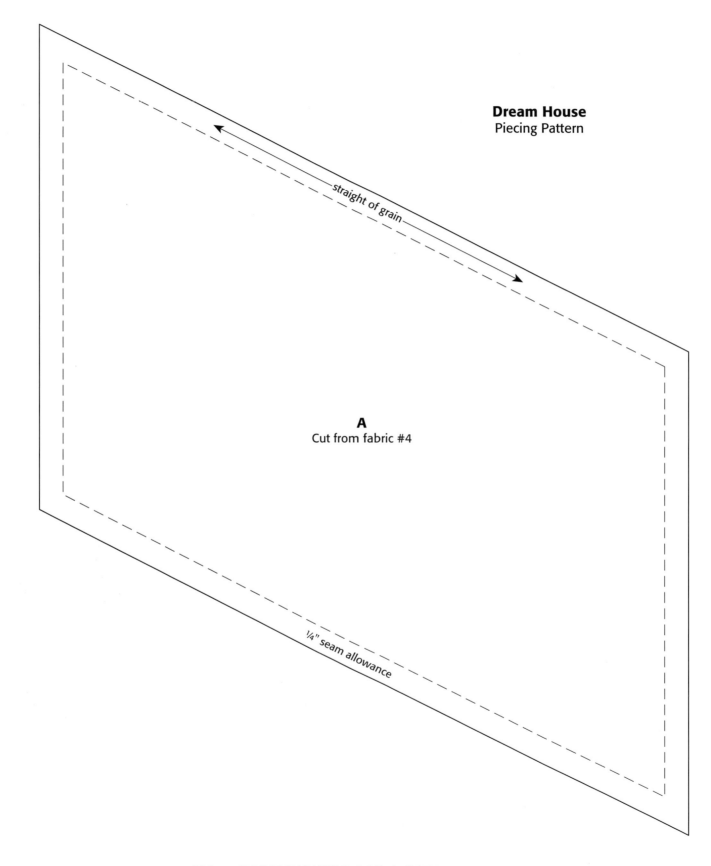

Dream House
Piecing Pattern

straight of grain

A
Cut from fabric #4

¼" seam allowance

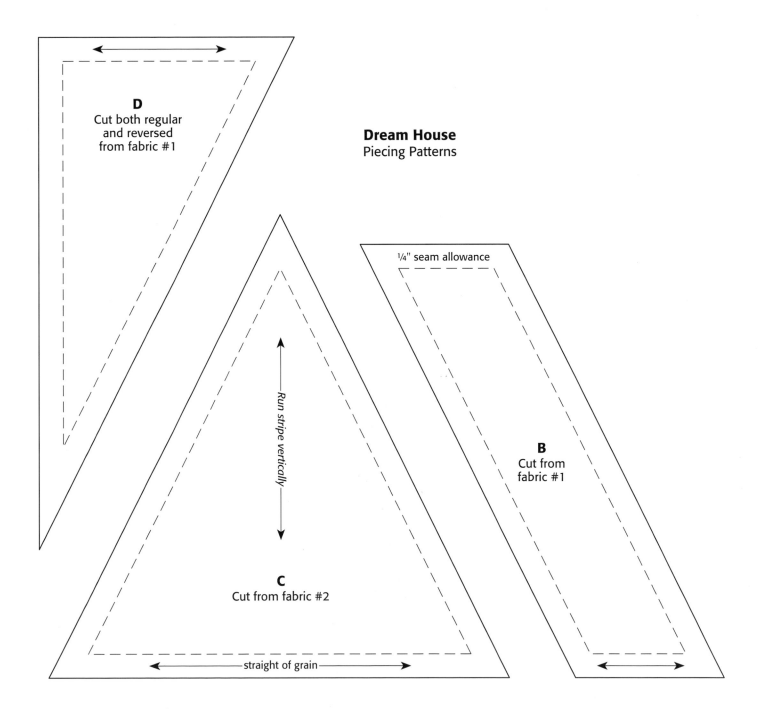

D
Cut both regular
and reversed
from fabric #1

Dream House
Piecing Patterns

¼" seam allowance

Run stripe vertically

B
Cut from
fabric #1

C
Cut from fabric #2

straight of grain

On Valentine's Day, traditional gifts such as heart-shaped chocolates, sentimental note cards, and delicate flowers provide a lovely means to honor loved ones too treasured to go unnoticed. Capture a dear one's affections on Valentine's Day by crafting our fabric confection—"Sweetheart Trellis." Its deceptively simple construction creates a cozy interplay of pattern, while the romantic heart appliqués encourage nestling under a quilt too pretty to hide when the holiday is done.

Lovers' Tart

INGREDIENTS FOR TART SHELL

1¼ cups flour

1 teaspoon salt

1 tablespoon sugar

¼ pound (1 stick) cold, unsalted butter, cut into small pieces

3 to 4 tablespoons ice water

INGREDIENTS FOR TART FILLING

Tart shell (see ingredients above)

1 cup blanched almonds, sliced

1 cup heavy cream

1 cup sugar

¼ teaspoon salt

1 tablespoon plus 2 teaspoons Grand Marnier

Zest of 1 orange

½ cup dried cranberries

To prepare the tart shell, combine flour, salt, and sugar in food processor. Add butter and process until mixture is crumbly, about 10 to 15 seconds. Processing in short pulses, gradually add ice water drop by drop through feed tube until dough comes together (no longer than 30 seconds). Turn dough onto plastic wrap, form into a disk, and refrigerate for 30 minutes.

On a floured surface, roll chilled dough into a circle large enough for a 9" tart pan with removable bottom and press into pan. Freeze for 30 minutes.

Preheat oven to 375 degrees. Remove tart shell from freezer, and use a fork to prick bottom of shell in several places. Partially bake tart shell for 15 minutes; remove from oven and allow to cool. Reduce oven temperature to 350°.

Combine almonds, cream, sugar, salt, and Grand Marnier in a saucepan. Cook over medium heat until sugar dissolves, about 10–15 minutes, stirring constantly. Stir in orange zest and remove mixture from heat. Place cranberries around outer edges of partially baked tart shell and pour mixture into shell. Bake until set and caramel colored, approximately 30 minutes. Let tart cool slightly and remove from pan.

YIELD: 8 SERVINGS.

Sweetheart Trellis

SWEETHEART TRELLIS
by Suzette Halferty, Carnation, Washington, 2000. Quilted by Sarah A. Yoder, Charm, Ohio.

FINISHED QUILT SIZE: 58½" x 58½"
FINISHED BLOCK SIZE: 16" SQUARE

MATERIALS

44"-wide fabric

- 1½ yd. rose print for blocks, appliqués, and inner border
- 2 yds. floral print for blocks, appliqués, and outer border
- 1¼ yds. yellow print for blocks and middle border
- 3¾ yds. fabric for backing
- 26" x 26" square of fabric for bias binding
- 64" x 64" piece of lightweight batting

CUTTING

All measurements include ¼"-wide seam allowances.

From the rose print, cut:
- 9 squares, each 7½" x 7½", for block centers
- 9 squares, each 4¼" x 4¼". Cut each square twice diagonally to make 36 triangles for blocks.
- 6 strips, each 2½" x 44", for inner border

From the floral print, cut:
- 18 squares, each 5⅞" x 5⅞". Cut each square once diagonally to make 36 triangles for blocks.
- 36 strips, each 3¾" x 7½", for blocks
- 6 strips, each 2½" x 44", for outer border

From the yellow print, cut:
- 36 strips, each 1½" x 7½", for blocks
- 36 strips, each 1½" x 4", for blocks
- 36 strips, each 1½" x 5", for blocks
- 6 strips, each 1½" x 44", for middle border

NOTE: *Refer to "Quiltmaking Basics" on pages 119–127 for guidance as needed with all basic quiltmaking techniques.*

MAKING THE BLOCKS

YOU'LL NEED 9 Sweetheart blocks for this quilt. A lovely trellis setting is created when the blocks are joined together. Larger rose-colored hearts are appliquéd over the block intersections.

1. Sew a 7½" rose-print square, and 2 each of the floral-print triangles, the 3¾" x 7½" floral strips, and the 1½" x 7½" yellow-print strips to construct a block unit as shown. Press seams toward the center square. Make 9.

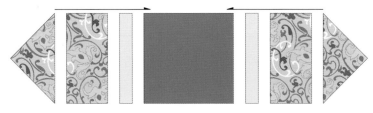

Make 9.

2. Sew a rose-print triangle, a 1½" x 4" yellow-print strip, and a 1½" x 5" yellow-print strip to construct a corner unit as shown. Press seams toward the triangle. Do not trim the excess strip length until the block is completed. Make 36.

Make 36.

3. Sew a floral-print triangle, a 3¾" x 7½" floral-print strip, and a 1½" x 7½" yellow-print strip to make a vertical row as shown. Press seams toward the triangle. Make 18.

Make 18.

4. Sew a corner unit from step 2 to opposite sides of each unit from step 3 as shown. Press seams toward the corner units. Make 18.

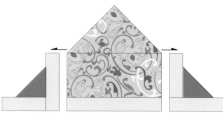

Make 18.

5. Sew each unit from step 1 between 2 units from step 4. Press seams toward the center unit.

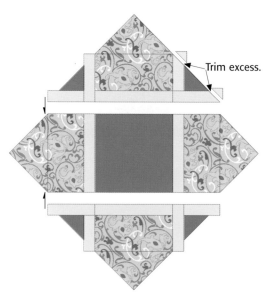

Trim excess.

Make 9.

6. Use a rotary cutter and quilter's ruler to trim the excess yellow strips, and to square blocks to 16½" x 16½".

7. Use the patterns on page 118 to make templates for appliqué pieces A and B. Trace the templates to cut 9 of piece A from the floral print and 4 of piece B from the rose print. Set the B appliqué pieces aside for now.

8. Appliqué a piece A in the rose-print center square in each Sweetheart block.

ASSEMBLING THE QUILT

1. Arrange the blocks in 3 horizontal rows of 3 blocks each. Sew the blocks into rows, pinning carefully to match the "trellis" strips. Press seams in opposite directions from row to row. Sew the rows together, and press.

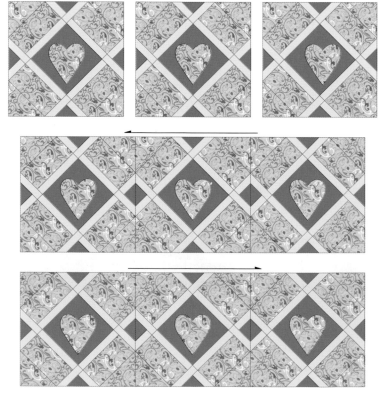

Assembly Diagram

2. Refer to the color photo on page 114, and appliqué a piece B over each of the intersections of the Sweetheart blocks.

3. Refer to step 3 and step 4 of "Assembling the Quilt" on page 100 to assemble 4 border units using the 2½" x 44" rose-print inner border strips, the 1½" x 44" yellow-print middle border strips, and the 2½" x 44" floral-print border strips. Press seams as desired. Trim, pin, and sew the border units to the quilt. Miter the corners (see page 122).

FINISHING

1. Mark the quilt top with a design of your choice.

2. Layer the quilt top with batting and backing; baste.

3. Hand or machine quilt as desired.

4. Trim the backing and batting even with the edges of the quilt top. Cut 2¼"-wide bias strips from the 26" square of binding fabric, for a total of approximately 250" of bias binding. Sew the binding to the quilt.

5. Make and attach a label to your quilt.

Sweetheart Trellis
Appliqué Patterns

Appliqué patterns do not include seam allowance.

B
Cut 4

A
Cut 9

THIS SECTION INCLUDES tips for completing a quilt with confidence and pride. What we suggest works well for us but is by no means the only way to accomplish the job. If a technique is new to you, try it; you might find that you incorporate the technique into your quiltmaking process from now on.

Bias Squares

MANY QUILT PATTERNS contain squares made from two contrasting half-square triangles. The short sides of the triangles are on the straight grain of the fabric while the long sides are on the bias. These are called bias squares. Using a bias-strip piecing method, you can easily sew and cut bias squares. This technique is especially useful for small bias squares, where pressing after stitching usually distorts the shape (and sometimes burns fingers). An easy way to cut bias squares for a scrappy-quilt look is to use 8" squares of fabric. For quilts with bias squares that are all cut from the same fabrics, use larger pieces. Measurements are included in the quilt directions.

NOTE: *All directions in this book give the cut size for bias squares; the finished size after stitching will be ½" smaller.*

1. Layer the two pieces of fabric stated in project directions, right sides facing up, and make a 45° diagonal cut beginning in one corner.

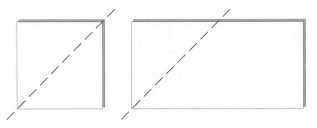

2. Cut into strips, measuring from the previous diagonal cut. Measurements are included in the quilt directions.

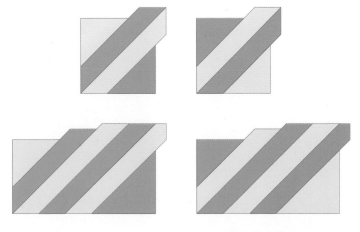

3. Stitch the strips together using ¼"-wide seam allowances. Be sure to align the strips so the lower edge and one adjacent edge form straight lines. Press seams toward the darker fabric.

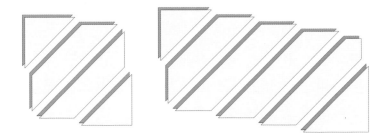

(continued on page 120)

4. Begin cutting at the lower left corner. Align the 45° mark of a Bias Square® ruler on the seam line. Each bias square will require 4 cuts. The first and second cuts are along the side and top edge. They remove the bias square from the rest of the fabric. Make these cuts slightly larger than the correct size.

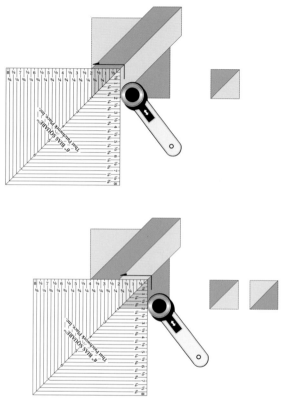

Align 45° mark on seam line and cut first 2 sides.

5. The third and fourth cuts are made along the remaining 2 sides. They align the diagonal and trim the bias square to the correct size. To make the cuts, turn the segment and place the Bias Square ruler on the opposite 2 sides, aligning the required measurements on both sides of the cutting guide and the 45° mark on the seam. Cut the remaining 2 sides of the bias squares.

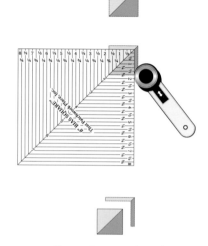

Turn cut segments and cut opposite 2 sides.

6. Continue cutting bias squares from each unit in this manner, working from left to right and from bottom to top, until you have cut bias squares from all usable fabric.

Fusible-Web Appliqué

THIS IS A time-saving technique that allows you to appliqué in a fraction of the time required for more traditional methods. Some of the projects in this book have instructions calling specifically for fusible-web appliqué, but with a little preplanning, any of the appliqué patterns can be adapted for the fusible-web technique. Keep in mind that you will probably wish to launder your picnic quilts, so be sure to follow the manufacturer's instructions carefully. Reserve fusible appliqués for small accents and/or secure the edges with stitching (step 5).

1. Prepare the pieces for appliqué by tracing the shapes on the paper side of fusible web. Patterns designed specifically for fusible-web appliqué have already been reversed. If you are adapting a pattern intended for traditional, stitched appliqué, you'll need to reverse the pattern before tracing.

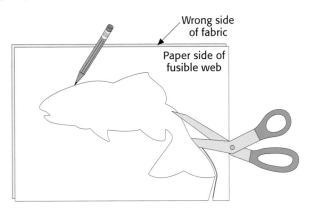

Wrong side of fabric

Paper side of fusible web

2. Using a dry (no steam) iron, follow the manufacturer's instructions and fuse the webbing to the wrong side of the fabric.

3. Cut on the drawn line and remove the paper.

4. Fuse the pieces to the background block or border.

5. To secure the appliqués more permanently to the fabric, finish the edges with hand or machine stitches such as those shown on page 122.

Bias-Strip Appliqué

SOME OF THE projects in this book include curved appliqué vines, which require strips cut on the bias of the fabric. Here is a simple technique for making easy-to-appliqué bias strips.

1. Cut bias strips according to the measurements indicated in the quilt directions. Refer to page 125, steps 1 and 2 for guidance as needed.

2. Fold each bias strip in half, wrong sides together, and stitch ⅛" from the long raw edges to form a tube. Press the tube so that the seam is centered on the tube's back side.

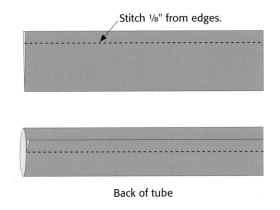

Stitch ⅛" from edges.

Back of tube

3. Place the bias tube on the background fabric, forming the desired shape. Pin (or baste) and stitch in place.

Embroidery Stitches

THESE ARE THE embroidery stitches suggested for some of the projects in this book. All may be adapted for finishing the edges of fusible-web appliqués (see page 120).

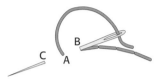

Outline or Backstitch

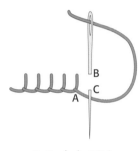

Buttonhole Stitch

Mitered Corners

1. To find the border length of one side of the quilt, measure through the center of the quilt top from edge to edge. To this measurement, add 2 times the border width (included in quilt directions); then add 2" to 3" extra to allow for the mitered corner's 45° angle. Repeat to find the border length for the remaining 3 sides, and cut borders to these measurements. If multiple border strips are planned, piece these together into a border unit.

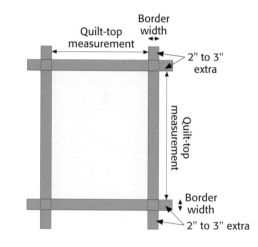

2. For one side of the quilt top, fold a border strip in half to find the center. Match the center of the border strip to the center of the edge on the quilt top. Pin the border in place, and start and end stitching ¼" from each corner of the quilt top. Repeat for the remaining 3 sides.

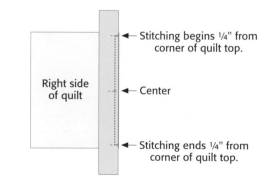

3. Arrange a corner of the quilt on an ironing board, crossing one border over the other at a 90° angle.

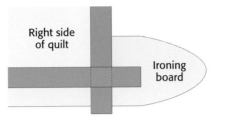

4. Turn under the overlapping (top) border, making a 45°-angle fold; press. This is the stitching line.

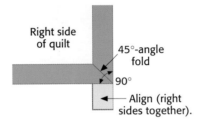

5. Fold the quilt, right sides together, matching borders at the corner. Pin to secure. Stitch on the pressed crease, backstitching at the outside edge and corner. Take care to keep the seam allowances out of the way.

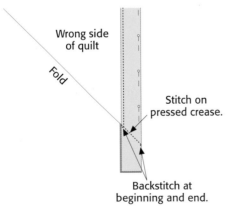

6. Trim the mitered seam allowances to ¼"; press to one side. Repeat for the remaining corners.

Layering the Quilt

BACKING

IF YOUR quilt is wider than 42", you will need to piece the back, although occasionally you can find fabric in extra-wide widths. Keep the seams to a minimum—quilting through them can be difficult. If you need to piece the backing, press the seams open. When choosing a fabric for your quilt backing, remember that solids or subtle prints show off your quilting stitches, while busy prints tend to hide them.

BASTING

BEFORE YOU quilt your layers together, baste them. You will find that a good basting job allows you to use any method of quilting that you find comfortable. To baste the layers, first press the backing. Place it wrong side up on a large table or other clean, flat surface. Secure the backing with masking tape or clips, gently pulling the fabric so that it lies taut. Center a piece of batting over the backing. Finish the "sandwich" by centering the quilt top right side up over the two layers.

Pin through all layers to secure if desired. With a thread of contrasting color, baste a square grid from the center out, in rows placed a maximum of 3" apart. (Baste only the portion of the quilt that lies on the table surface, and reposition the quilt as needed.) Take long running stitches until you reach the end of the grid, then take a backstitch and remove the needle.

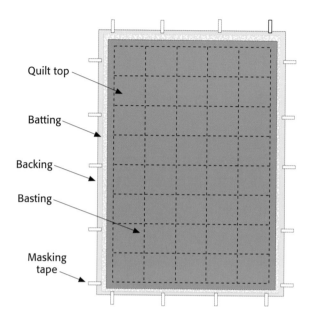

Quilt top

Batting

Backing

Basting

Masking tape

Hand Quilting

ONCE YOU HAVE basted your quilt layers, you are ready to quilt. For hand quilting, you may use a hoop or a frame to support your work and keep it taut. If you prefer, you may simply quilt in your lap. Experiment to find the method you prefer.

1. Choose a sturdy needle (size 10 or 12 Between, for example), 100 percent–cotton quilting thread, and a thimble for the middle finger of your quilting hand. Cut an 18" length of thread, thread the needle, and make a small knot at the end of the thread.

2. Work from the center of the quilt outward. Insert the needle through the quilt top, running it between the layers about 1" from where you plan to begin stitching. Bring the needle out on the stitching line and tug gently on the thread to pull the knot between the layers.

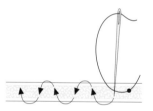

3. Take a small backstitch through all 3 layers; then take small, even running stitches—2 or 3 at a time—rocking the needle up and down with each stitch. Keep your other hand underneath the quilt, feeling the needle go through the layers and pushing it back up, also in a rocking motion. Remove basting threads as you go.

4. When you near the end of the length of thread, make a knot close to your work. Insert the needle into the hole where it last emerged, and slide it between the layers for approximately 1", bringing it out the top. Gently pull the knot inside the layers. Carefully clip the remaining thread tail close to the quilt top.

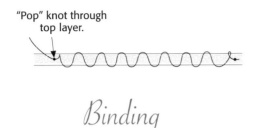

"Pop" knot through top layer.

Binding

THE QUILTS IN this book call for double-fold French binding made from 2¼"-wide bias strips. The quilt directions tell you how much fabric you will need.

After quilting, trim the excess batting and backing even with the edge of the quilt top. A rotary cutter and long ruler will ensure accurate, straight edges. Baste all three layers together along the outside edges. (If you have a walking foot, you can do this with a larger-than-normal stitch on your sewing machine.)

To cut bias strips for binding, follow these steps:

1. Align the 45° marking of a Bias Square along the selvage and place a long ruler's edge against it. Make the first cut.

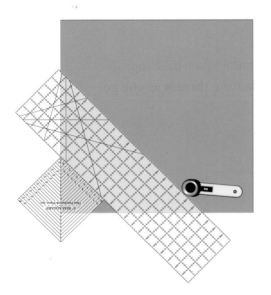

2. Measure the width of the strip (2¼") from the cut edge of the fabric. Cut along the edge with the ruler. Continue cutting until you have the number of strips necessary to achieve the required binding length.

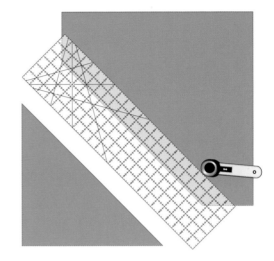

Sometimes a 24"-long ruler may be too short for some of the cuts. After making several cuts, carefully fold the fabric over itself so that the bias edges are even. Continue to cut the bias strips.

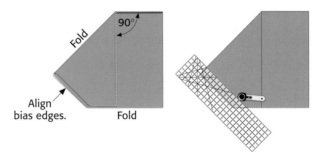

Fold   90°

Align bias edges.   Fold

Follow these steps to bind the edges:

1. Stitch bias strips together, offsetting them as shown. Press seams open.

4. Starting on one side of the quilt (not a corner), stitch the binding to the quilt. Use a ¼"-wide seam allowance. Begin stitching 1" to 2" from the start of the binding. Stop stitching ¼" from the first corner and backstitch.

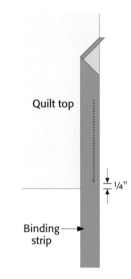

Quilt top

Binding strip

¼"

5. Turn the quilt to prepare for sewing along the next edge. Fold the binding away from the quilt; then fold the binding again to place it along the second edge of the quilt. This fold creates an angled pleat at the corner.

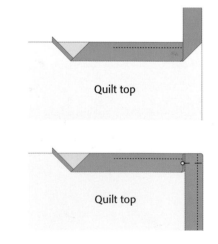

Quilt top

Quilt top

2. Fold the strip in half lengthwise, wrong sides together, and press.

Fold line

Right side

Wrong side

3. Unfold the binding at one end and turn under ¼" at a 45° angle as shown.

Fold line

6. Stitch from the fold of the binding along the second edge of the quilt top, stopping ¼" from the corner as before. Repeat the stitching and mitering process on the remaining edges and corners of the quilt.

7. When you reach the beginning of the binding, cut the end 1" longer than needed, and tuck the end inside the beginning. Finish stitching the binding to the quilt.

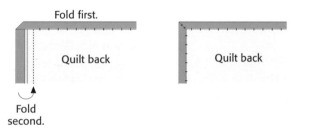

Quilt top

8. Turn the binding over the raw edges to the back side of the quilt. Blindstitch the binding in place so that the folded edge covers the machine stitching. Fold the binding at each corner to form a miter on the back of the quilt, and stitch in place.

Fold first.

Quilt back   Quilt back

Fold
second.

Acknowledgments

OUR SINCERE APPRECIATION to the following people and companies, who provided exactly what we needed.

Miller's Dry Goods and Amanda Miller's Quilting Service, especially Elsie Mast, Emma Raber, Emma Shetler, Leanna Troyer, and Miriam Yoder; Amish Quilting Service, Millicent Agnor and Associates—especially Elizabeth Hostetler, Suzie Hostetler, Treva Mast, Hattie Schrock, Rose Schwartz, and Sarah A. Yoder; Alvina Nelson in Salina, Kansas, for her lovely hand quilting; Frankie Schmidt of Dizzy Stitches for machine quilting; All who helped stitch: Cleo Nollette, Nancy Sweeney, and Becky Hansen; Beth Kovich for use of her casserole carrier pattern; The homeowners who generously opened their homes and gardens: Dorothy and Jerry Stansberry, Chris and Gary Todd, Cherry and Terry Jarvis, Sheri and Lauren Defaccio; The businesses which allowed us to photograph on their premises: Purple Haze Lavender Farm · 180 Bell Bottom Road · Sequim, Washington Mike and Jadyne Reichner, proprietors; Jones Tree Farm · 1795 NE Sawdust Hill Road · Poulsbo, Washington Rainbow Inn · La Conner, Washington Tom, Patsy, Bruce, and Laurceo Squires, proprietors; City of Woodinville Recreation Fields; Bothell Landing and the Bothell Parks and Recreation Commission; All those who provided wonderful props: Terry Jarvis for the antique car; Carol Swanson for the bees skep; Marsha and Jack Seip for the Hawkeye picnic basket; Donna Lever for the wicker picnic basket and seed packet invitations; Mike Gunderson for the antique truck; Mills Music in Bothell, Washington, for the cello and French horn; Nadine Stephenson for the antique picnic baskets; Suzette's friends and neighbors, who provided friendship and support: Nancy and Gary Sweeney, Becky and Bruce Hansen, Sally and Gary Todd, Lois and Fred Bereswill, Megan and Ron Bluher, Polly and Jeff Hutchison, Kathleen and Marty Kearns, David and Marissa Kern, and Larry and Susan Nakatsu; and Megan Jane Martin for all of her boots, umbrellas, and raincoats.